ON GOOD MANAGEMENT

Roland Berger
School of Strategy and Economics

BURKHARD SCHWENKER · MARIO MÜLLER-DOFEL

ON GOOD MANAGEMENT

The Corporate Lifecycle

An essay and interviews with
Franz Fehrenbach, Jürgen Hambrecht,
Wolfgang Reitzle and Alexander Rittweger

Springer Gabler

SERIES EDITORS

DR. KATRIN VERNAU
Partner
Roland Berger Strategy Consultants
Dean
Roland Berger School
of Strategy and Economics

KLAUS FUEST
Principal
Roland Berger Strategy Consultants
Roland Berger School
of Strategy and Economics

DR. CHRISTIAN KRYS
Senior Expert
Roland Berger Strategy Consultants
Roland Berger School
of Strategy and Economics

AUTHORS

PROF. DR. BURKHARD SCHWENKER
CEO
Roland Berger Strategy Consultants
Chairman
Roland Berger School
of Strategy and Economics

MARIO MÜLLER-DOFEL
Journalist and Communication Trainer
Dialektik for Business

ISBN 978-3-658-02877-0 ISBN 978-3-658-02878-7 (eBook)
DOI 10.1007/ 978-3-658-02878-7

Die Deutsche Nationalbibliothek verzeichnet diese Publikation in der Deutschen Nationalbibliografie; detaillierte bibliografische Daten sind im Internet über http://dnb.d-nb.de abrufbar.

Springer Gabler

Lektorat: Stefanie A. Winter
Layout und Satz: workformedia | Frankfurt am Main | München

Gedruckt auf säurefreiem und chlorfrei gebleichtem Papier

Springer Gabler ist eine Marke von Springer DE. Springer DE ist Teil der Fachverlagsgruppe Springer Science+Business Media
www.springer-gabler.de

"FOR THAT MAN WHO,
WHEN TIMES ARE UNCERTAIN,
IS FALTERING IN SPIRIT,
ONLY INCREASES THE EVIL."

JOHANN WOLFGANG VON GOETHE

CONTENTS

PREFACE: DEDICATION TO AN ENTREPRENEUR

The idea for this book grew out of a challenge: the challenge of finding a suitable present to mark Roland Berger's 75th birthday. One thought immediately sprang to mind: maybe a book about lifecycles. Why? Because few people can lay claim to a life as successful as Roland Berger's. He is the successful founder of a successful consulting firm that has remained successful to this day, 45 years after its inception. It is also the only consulting firm of German origin that competes with the world's biggest and best.

Stories such as that of Roland Berger are inextricably interwoven with a series of skills and factors that, as we will see, can determine whether a company (or an entrepreneur) succeeds or fails in the course of its (or his or her) lifecycle:

- The first is having the right idea at the right time. When Roland Berger founded the company that bears his name in 1967, few people in Germany had heard of management consulting. Where it existed at all, it was American consulting firms that were getting the ball rolling.
- The second is sufficient creativity to communicate new solutions or strategies convincingly. Roland Berger himself points to the build-up of tourism group TUI in the 1970s as his breakthrough project. To this day, the same success factors – marketing, a systematic approach, networking, collaboration and size – have lost none of their validity.
- The third is the courage to take risks in order to occupy a position. The word "entrepreneur" means someone who wants to be enterprising, who wants to do something. That is one of the core attitudes I learned from Roland Berger right from the outset.

◆ The fourth is the ability to convince people – initially to convince them of your ideas ("the German alternative to the American style of consulting") and later to convince them of the need to continue growing rapidly – and then of the need to get involved.
◆ The fifth – another vital skill in the course of a company's lifecycle – is the ability to delegate and let go of things. In the history of the Roland Berger company, this capability is reflected in the transition from what was once a startup with one owner and one decision-maker to a partnership with many owners governed by a philosophy of meritocracy. In my personal relationship with Roland Berger, this was shown in his handing the reins over to me, initially when I succeeded him as CEO and later when I became chairman of the company. I did not realize how difficult and challenging handing things over can be until, two years ago, I too stood down from my role as CEO and in turn passed on the baton to my successor, Martin Wittig.[1]

These experiences alone would be enough to fill a book. To describe the history and lifecycle of our company merely in terms of anecdotes and recollections would, however, do a grave injustice to the intellectual capabilities of Roland Berger. That is why I took the idea a step further: The book was to be about "good corporate management", with the concept of lifecycles both befitting the occasion and setting the framework.

The idea of a company's lifecycle also lends itself to the task in hand because, to my mind at least, the very concept is a contradiction in terms. On the one hand, it is intuitive. Companies are founded or products are developed. They are successful and grow until the market becomes saturated and then they "die". Because there are distinct phases and because these phases are predictable, it is possible to think in advance about what success factors are critical to which phase – and about what forms of management (or which leaders) are the most suitable in each case. As I see it, this is precisely the reason why management literature has for decades been packed with discussions about lifecycle concepts, despite the fact that these concepts are often little more than common sense.

On the other hand – and hence the fascination for me personally – lifecycle models make an implicit basic assumption that I believe is incorrect: that of a fixed, predetermined lifespan. Companies are not biological entities. Their death is not predestined by fate. Rather than looking for the style of management that is best suited to this or that phase, we should actually be looking for leaders and strategies that can help a firm break out of the regular pattern of phases. Precisely this search leads us to the questions that are most relevant for "good management": How do we grow quickly without spinning out of control? How do we escape the saturation that appears inevitable and, instead, continue to grow? Or if that doesn't work in the long run, how do we know whether the much-vaunted relaunch, the "reinvention" of a company, is at all feasible? And if it isn't, where do we find the courage to prepare the ground for a rich harvest before decline sets in? For me, the question of whether to reboot or head for the exit is one of the most exciting in a company's lifecycle. My answer is that genuine entrepreneurship and good management can also show themselves for what they are by soberly deciding to beat the retreat and sell.

The inherent contradictions in the lifecycle concept also reflect the diametric opposites which good management must deal with:

- As managers we know that the future is complex and, above all, uncertain. Yet precisely because this is so, the people in our companies feel a need for security that we must factor into our considerations.
- We know from painful experience that trends and numbers can no longer be relied upon. Yet we still have to plan, do our sums and decide about investments.
- We know that an interdisciplinary mindset is the only way to stay abreast of the complex world we live in. Yet at the same time, expert knowledge and practical experience are necessary if we are to properly steer our companies' day-to-day business.

In my opinion, this circle can be squared with a piece of good news: Corporate management is once again becoming more direct, more personal, more entrepreneurial. It can no longer hide behind models, concepts and techniques. On the contrary, it demands personality, courage, the ability to think and reflect, and a system of proven values. Managers need to have convictions: They must nail their colors to the mast. That is why we prefixed this book with a quote from Goethe: "For that man who, when times are uncertain, is faltering in spirit, only increases the evil."

This book represents a personal opinion. It is not an academic treatise. It is an essay, an at times very personal meditation, if you like, on what makes good management today. Its purpose is to take stock of where we are at and, ideally, provide orientation for the way forward. Thinking about the idea of lifecycles – the conceptual framework for this book – has also shown me how little existing concepts reflect the conditions that are faced by company managers today. For this reason, the book also attempts to stake out a new, contemporary lifecycle concept.

We don't want these considerations to remain purely conceptual, of course. The second part of the book brings together a series of in-depth interviews with outstanding company founders and business leaders: Franz Fehrenbach, Dr. Jürgen Hambrecht, Professor Wolfgang Reitzle and Alexander Rittweger. These individuals have become synonymous with excellent corporate management, farsighted vision and sociopolitical commitment. In the course of their careers, they have mastered a whole battery of challenges in the lifecycle of the companies they represent. They willingly agreed to share their experience and insights, and to corroborate – or, on occasion, contradict – my own musings. For this I am sincerely grateful. Incidentally, they are all also long-standing associates and close friends of Roland Berger himself, a fact that neatly rounds off the fundamental motivation for writing this book.

The interviews were prepared by Mario Müller-Dofel and conducted by an experienced business journalist whose professionalism and unerring sensitivity have translated deep insights into an exciting read, and to whom I owe a debt of gratitude. Thanks are also due to my colleagues Klaus Fuest, Professor Torsten Oltmanns and Dr. Tobias Raffel. As in my other publications, their creative ideas, first-class research and stimulating discussions played a very substantial part in bringing this project to fruition. Last, but by no means least, my thanks go to Dr. Katherine Nölling, whose exceptional skill, tenacity and powers of persuasion ensured that the book was finished on time. Birthdays always come around faster than you thought.

This book is dedicated – as a birthday present – to my mentor and guide Roland Berger, who, over the years, has also become my friend.

Dear Roland, congratulations on your 75th birthday!

HAMBURG, NOVEMBER 2012,
PROFESSOR BURKHARD SCHWENKER

1. THE CHALLENGES OF GOOD MANAGEMENT

1.1 WHAT SHOULD INFLUENCE HOW WE THINK ABOUT GOOD MANAGEMENT

Why yet another book about corporate management? Scarcely any aspect of management doctrine has triggered such an avalanche of writings. Over the past ten years alone, no fewer than 23,943 new books on the subject have appeared in German or English. That's 2,394 books a year, or more than ten on every working day.[2] One would think that everything worth thinking has already been thought.

Yet the world is changing at an ever more rapid pace. "Truths" that had become flesh and blood are suddenly unmasked as error. As recently as a decade ago, who would have thought that the Internet would revolutionize the retail industry or that green technology would shape our growth trajectory? Or that Germany would, once and for all, pull the plug on nuclear power? Or that China would emerge as the world's biggest net exporter, prompting the US to herald the advent of the "Pacific Age"? And who would have thought that the financial markets would spiral completely out of control, plunging us into one of the most profound global economic crises since the 1930s?

In a lead story entitled "The Nightmare of the Alpha Dogs", Manager Magazin, a respected German-language business periodical, asserts that "Risks are growing more dramatic, markets more volatile, technological leaps more gigantic and global entanglements more complex by the day."[3] While that may be stretching the point a little too far, brain researcher Gerald Hüther is nonetheless right, in the same context, to make the following observation: "Everyone in politics and business knows that we stand on the verge of a transformation process, that something is going to have to change completely."[4]

The fact that our notion of corporate strategy must change completely has already been underscored by my brief list of the fundamental changes that have taken place over the past ten years. And the list is not even exhaustive. If it is no longer possible to paint a realistic picture of future developments, then it also makes little sense to calculate a detailed strategic plan for the next ten years, or to base investment decisions primarily on quantitative computations. No, we need to find other ways. I see three points that should influence how we think about good management – and that show why thinking about good management from time to time is always a valuable exercise.

FIRST: CORPORATE MANAGEMENT IS GROWING MORE COMPLEX

People often contradict me when I make this argument. The world, they say, has always been complex, the demands placed on management always exacting. Nor are upheavals a new phenomenon. There is also the view that the absence of "always-on communication" used to lead to much greater information asymmetries. While there is nothing wrong with all these assertions, there is a very definite scientific distinction between the terms "complicated" and "complex".[5] Many of the above factors do indeed make a system more complicated. Only one thing, however, leads to genuine complexity, and that is uncertainty.

In the context of corporate planning, uncertainty has become virtually ubiquitous these days. We will later examine why national economic forecasts no longer constitute a valid planning framework. For now, suffice it to say that, when research institutes constantly have to adjust their growth forecasts – which they did six times in 2011 alone – the outcomes can never serve as a reliable basis for corporate planning. When the DAX share index fluctuates between 7,000 and 5,000 points in a short space of time, it is only fair to speak of pronounced volatility. When the scheduled lifespan of nuclear power plants is first extended and then suddenly curtailed due to a political volte-face, conditions can no longer be said to be stable. To put it bluntly: The pace of change is picking up, it is becoming ever more difficult to maintain a clear overview of events and, as people are no longer sure what is going on, uncertainty is increasing.

This has several implications for good management: It means that business acumen is once again coming to the fore as predictability is on the wane. It means that it is important for leaders to know where they stand, to be able to make up their own mind about the future and not to go running after every trend that crosses their path. It means that the ability to reflect on things and the willingness to think in interdisciplinary terms is at a premium. After all, if we as entrepreneurs want to successfully overcome uncertainty, we need to look beyond our own backyard and build bridges. Bridges, for example, between the following:

- Business management concepts (What is the right way to organize the company? How do you gain lasting competitive advantages?)
- Economic concepts (How does growth work? What models is it based upon? How is economic policy changing?)
- Sociopolitical concepts (What values are important? What attitudes will shape future societies?)
- Geopolitical concepts (Where do security risks exist? How will countries and regions develop? What significance will regional alliances have?)

Careful reflection and interdisciplinary thinking don't just materialize out of thin air, however. We must point the training of our managers in this direction, and we must do the same with our day-to-day work: Where do we look for new ideas? How do we find room for the creative freedom to sketch pictures of the future? How do we populate a management team in a way that maximizes interdisciplinary influences? At the same time, we must reassess the tools of the management trade. Which brings me to my second point.

SECOND: THE VALIDITY OF OUR TRADITIONAL STRATEGY AND PLANNING CONCEPTS IS ERODING

This is happening not for lack of concepts. Until the early 1990s, diversification drove corporate strategic thinking. This period was followed by a concentration on "core competencies", combined with every conceivable variation on the theme of reengineering and/or corporate transformation. The New Economy ushered in the "deconstruction" of the value chain, later giving way once again to a concentration on core business. And diversification too is back on the menu today – at least as a side dish. Somewhere along the line, we have also seen trends toward the centralization and then the decentralization or distribution of corporate management.

Right now, centralization seems to be on the rebound – although I hope not, as I will discuss later on.

This constant stream of alternative strategy concepts leads many to conclude that corporate management is vulnerable to fashion fads, masterminded not least by consulting firms eager for new business. I may not be objective on this point, but I do not believe this is so. Why? Because almost every one of the concepts listed above had its rightful place at the time and given the prevailing conditions. Today, the problem is rather that such stable conditions no longer exist. This being the case, good management also involves recognizing when a concept no longer applies – and having the courage to go against the flow of both public and expert opinion and switch to a new concept. Or switch to an old one that might be just the right thing for the current situation.

What is true of strategy concepts is equally true of our planning tools. The experience curve is a good example of what I mean. We have all learned that the unit cost of a product can be reduced by 20% to 30% every time the cumulative production volume is doubled. That is a very useful thing to know when investing in expansion, setting prices and projecting cashflow. At least, it is useful at times when growth rates are high and your business environment is stable. If sales of a product are growing at a rate of 15% per annum, doubling the volume takes just five years. Even at a rate of 10%, it still only takes seven years. Both are manageable periods for planning purposes. But what do you do when your rate of growth shrinks to just 3%, meaning it will take 20 years to double your sales, or when new technology suddenly paves the way for completely new production methods? Or when growth of any sort is so volatile that reliable growth forecasts are simply no longer possible? In such circumstances, what used to be useful cost information is worse than obsolete: It can actually be dangerous.

The same goes for many modern methods of corporate finance. I know from my own experience how tempting it can be to adapt the analytical elegance of the capital asset pricing model in order to calculate the cost of capital. But what use is greater elegance and precision to me if the development of future cashflows – which this concept is supposed to analyze – is becoming increasingly uncertain? An incorrect estimate of cashflow development has worse consequences than a calculation of capital costs that was off the mark. Albert Einstein's famous saying is more valid today than ever before: "Not everything that can be counted counts, and not everything that counts can be counted."[6]

Of course, as far as good management is concerned, that doesn't mean that we should do without modern quantitative models and concepts entirely. Correctly applied, they can still help us reduce complexity and prepare decisions. What it does mean, however, is that we must think long and hard about when the analytical effort involved in these models is justified, and whether we have set our priorities correctly. Above all, it means that we must be more keenly aware of the assumptions and limitations that underpin such models. I do not believe that the financial crisis was driven by the complex algorithms that are used to design and put a value on derivatives. But I do believe that it was driven by users who did not know (or want to know) the assumptions and limitations inherent in these models.

We could say the same also applies to the shareholder value concepts that have substantially influenced our understanding of management since the 1980s. Again, there is nothing wrong in seeking to increase value and boost cashflow. But there is something wrong when we concentrate exclusively on finance and the capital markets. At the peak of the latest financial crisis, Jack Welch, former CEO of General Electric and perhaps the best-known proponent of the American-born shareholder value philosophy, acknowledged that: "On the face of it, shareholder value is the dumbest idea in the world. Shareholder value is a result, not a strategy (…). The main pillars are your employees, your customers and your products."[7]

Seen from this angle, my first two arguments about what should influence how we think about good management can be mapped onto an (admittedly oversimplified) "if-then" sequence:

- If trends are no longer reliable, then numbers will be of limited use as a basis for planning and decision making.
- If numbers cannot help us, then we must wave goodbye to the idea of wanting to quantify every entrepreneurial decision. What is useful, however, is a feel for technology, for what customers need and for underlying economic and sociopolitical developments.

◆ If the business environment is changing so fast, then short-termism will appear to be right. Only a long-term picture of the future can give orientation to the people in our companies.
◆ If the people in our companies are unsettled by complexity, then trust in the capabilities of management plays a pivotal role.

Underpinning this almost aphoristic summary is my third argument as to why we should rethink what good management means.

THIRD: WE NEED A NEW UNDERSTANDING OF WHAT MANAGEMENT MEANS

In the past – in the days before the Soviet Union imploded, before globalization and before the Internet – the world was content to work with the fiction of at least something like medium-term certainty. Today, however, we are confronted by fundamental doubts about the predictability of the future. In the past, clear, unambiguous statements – "this is our strategy", "that is our goal" – allowed us to reduce complexity and communicate a sense of security. In their place, uncertainty is now driving complexity and making clear statements impossible.

For me, communicating a sense of security is very important to good management. I believe every one of us has a deep longing for security – for a secure income, a safe job, solid career prospects, a future that we can visualize and look forward to. I see "org charts", for example, as symbolic of how we strive for this security and of the contradictions that are inherent in this striving today. On the one hand, we have known for years that we must be process-oriented in the way we run our companies, assigning tasks flexibly and avoiding structures that are cast in stone. Yet virtually every company still has an organization chart. Look, there's the little box with my name on it. That's my home. That's where I belong.

The challenge today is that no truly responsible manager is in a position to say how long any such org chart will remain valid. The same is true of supposedly reliable planning figures, which are likewise intended to convey a sense of security.

So we find ourselves in need of something new to replace the security we have lost. To my mind, this can only be anchored in the personality of managers and leaders. These days, no one can hide behind a number or a plan. Every manager must be able to explain their convictions and how they see the future. To paraphrase Joseph Schumpeter: Those who talk about their visions reveal the limits of their horizons. This is precisely the issue at stake: having a broad horizon – and having the courage to make it known. Managers communicate a sense of security and nurture trust by making it clear that they are willing and able to deal with complex situations, and by showing that they have sufficient integrity to tackle these situations in the best interests of the company and its people.

The good news is that this approach makes management more direct and personal. It becomes less technocratic, more accessible to people and closer to the business, clients and technology used. In other words, management becomes more entrepreneurial – more enterprising. The challenging news is that, on its own, this is not enough. Managers also need to cultivate an interdisciplinary mindset if political and social developments are to be factored into their business decisions. That is why analytical skills remain at a premium: For all the complexity that surrounds us, identifying patterns will be as necessary as ever in the future.

1.2 A SURVEY: WHY MANAGEMENT OFTEN FAILS

Are these challenging demands too much for top executives? In light of such complexity, is it possible for anyone to lead a company to success? What is certainly true – and we shall look at this more closely in the next chapter – is that not all companies are managed successfully. Failure is by no means uncommon. But what exactly goes wrong when companies fail? What management mistakes or behaviors lie at the root of the strategic errors and operational difficulties that can threaten the very survival of the modern enterprise? I posed the same questions to my fellow Partners at Roland Berger, asking them to list what they see as the seven most important reasons for failure and then prioritize them (7 being the most important, 1 the least important). Clustered on a qualitative basis and sorted by mean values, my survey produced the following result:

Mean	Problem area
5.2	Recognizing and mastering change
4.4	Managers' behavior and personalities
3.5	Mastery of operational tools

First the good news. Basic errors regarding how the tools of the trade are applied evidently play only a subordinate role in corporate failure. Under the heading "mastery of operational tools", I subsumed all answers relating to key company processes, primarily finance, controlling, human resources and marketing. Companies can, of course, fail because of a faulty capital structure or defective liquidity management, or because controllers fail to deliver transparent numbers as a solid basis for good decisions. Or because cash cows are overmilked while new marketing initiatives and ideas are ignored. Compared to other potential problem areas, however, fewer mistakes – or at least fewer dramatic ones – occur in these contexts.

Interestingly, missing or inadequate risk management systems scarcely seem to be a problem, except for in the finance industry. The same goes for ill-calibrated incentive systems. On the operational side, companies seem to have their house largely in order: Functional problems or mistakes seldom cause companies to fail. To put that another way: The efforts made in recent years to make corporate functions more professional and optimize processes have obviously had a powerful impact. Companies have become better as a result. I believe that is, in part, a huge compliment to the second- and third-tier managers who are usually responsible for the operational side of these undertakings.

At least when it comes to one decisive dimension, the picture at the very top – the top management level – is not quite as rosy. "Recognizing and mastering change" must surely be the most important job of top management. Yet it is precisely here that the Partners at Roland Berger see the principal reasons why companies fail. Typical mistakes, and behaviors that lead to mistakes, include the following (all of which are direct quotations from the survey):

◆ Early warning signals that indicate, say, changes on the market or in the technology are missed or intentionally hushed up.
◆ Regulatory and political influences on future corporate development are systematically underestimated.
◆ Changes affecting the market and customers are not analyzed and discussed sufficiently at board level.
◆ Business models are not subjected to critical reflection.
◆ People hold onto traditional and hitherto successful ways of doing things for too long.
◆ The courage to argue against conventional wisdom is lacking.
◆ Even where tangible changes are made, actions are too hesitant. Managers immerse themselves in action for action's sake and showmanship without doing anything concrete.
◆ There is no clear, compellingly communicated vision of change and strategy to achieve it.

None of these answers comes as a surprise. Nor is the resultant insight really new: It is not change itself that causes companies to fail but the inability to recognize change in good time and to respond to it courageously and energetically. What does come as a surprise is something completely different: Given the multiplicity of new early-warning instruments, the number of think tanks that are constantly churning out new future scenarios, the many corporate departments and, by no means least, the plethora of consultants providing strategic support to top management, it is hard to believe that "recognizing and mastering change" is really still such a huge problem.

The results of this survey remind me of the American historian Barbara Tuchman's remarkable analysis in her book "The March of Folly: from Troy to Vietnam." She concludes that gross strategic errors are attributable not to a lack of knowledge, nor to the absence of information signals, but to decision makers who fall at the hurdle of either their own ego and/or the institutional conditions that surround them.[8] Precisely this view is corroborated by the answers supplied by the Partners at Roland Berger and grouped together in the cluster "managers' behavior and personalities". These answers show why companies so often fail to master change.

Within this category, there are three main reasons why companies fail (quotations are from the survey):

◆ They fail because of personalities: "Alpha dogs who see themselves as infallible", "egotism, arrogance and hubris", a "lack of self-reflection".

◆ They fail because of an internal culture of "yes men": "Executive and supervisory board meetings are cozy little self-promotion gatherings", "a considerable amount of internal politicking", "no ability at the highest level to deal with conflicts", "a lack of entrepreneurship and willingness to take risks".

◆ They fail because of a lack of team orientation: "No ability to achieve buy in", "values are not lived out", "overweening personal ambition".

Unlike the findings of the survey for second- and third-tier management, the findings for top managers are not exactly flattering. Yet even if leading questions may have led to a negative selection that was possibly somewhat distorted – I had, after all, asked about reasons for failure – I am still convinced that we can legitimately draw at least one conclusion: The exacting conceptual demands identified in our discussion of growing uncertainty are accompanied by equally exacting personal demands.

1.3 THE SEARCH FOR A CONCEPTUAL FRAMEWORK

Being a good manager is clearly an ever more daunting challenge. That is not to say that everything is now new and different: The tasks to be resolved definitely don't change. US think tank "The Conference Board" has for years been asking top managers about their biggest challenges. Two challenges have consistently ranked among the top three mentioned:

◆ "Excellence in execution" (42.3% of all responses)

◆ "Sustained and steady growth" (38.8% of all responses)[9]

The question of how well business decisions are implemented – i.e. how quickly, rigorously and convincingly – loses none of its relevance over time. Neither does the question about realizing a stable growth trajectory.

Some years ago, I attempted to distill these challenges into something more tangible in a series of articles ("Schwenker's Strategy")[10] published in Handelsblatt, an influential German business daily. Together – Handelsblatt itself contributed portraits of major corporations – we identified five key questions to track down good management: What management and organizational structures facilitate successful global growth? How radically can and should a company change its business model? How do you guide employees through the turbulence inherent in this kind of transformation? Is focusing on core business really the best solution? And if not, how can a diversified group be well managed?

The series was published in 2005/2006, just six or seven years ago. In my opinion, while the key questions remain just as valid today, that is not true of all the answers. Our understanding of good management is changing. It has to change, because the conditions that surround it are changing too. But if the answers to the questions are different now, that raises another question: Is there a model that maps out the fundamental elements of "good management" in a way that lets us go through the relevant changes on a conceptual level step by step?

I have already touched on the view that the answers to fundamental strategy and management questions can sometimes be found by looking back to old concepts. Let me give an example: I believe that the profit impact of market strategies (or PIMS) concept popular in the 1970s and 80s still has a part to play, because the way in which market shares, quality and profitability relate to each other has profound implications for the running of a company.[11] Another example from the same period is Michael Porter's deliberations on the relationships between corporate strategies and industrial structures. These notions concern pivotal management issues: How do you manage when cost leadership is the central issue? And what do you differently if differentiation is essential?[12]

The same could be said of the insights presented by Tom Peters and Robert Waterman. In "In Search of Excellence", 30 years ago, they made it clear that it is important to be close to customers and technology, and that it is crucial to give employees a measure of entrepreneurial freedom.[13]

In preparing this discussion of good management, I have drawn on the concept of the "corporate lifecycle" for three main reasons:

◆ First, the basic idea is highly intuitive: Companies are founded, they grow, reach the limits of growth and either reinvent themselves or die.

◆ Second, the lifecycle model concerns itself with questions that are relevant for good management: How do you grow? How do you invent a new business model? How do you align an organization with a new business model? Which management skills are important in the process?

◆ Third, the model enables forecasts: If you know which phase you are in, you also know which one comes next and can prepare accordingly and in good time.

I believe that the lifecycle model helps us conceptualize the principles of good management as they apply to different situations and phases, and go through them step by step. This is all the more true because the model also factors in the uncertainty we have to deal with in this day and age. As Charlie Chaplin said: "At the crossroads of life there are no signposts."[14]

Having said that, looking at the familiar lifecycle models, I have found that they suffer from the same problem as many other strategic concepts: They no longer truly fit reality. Change is simply happening too quickly. New technology is breaking the mold of known phases. Forecasting the next phase is no longer as easy as it once was.

In the next chapter I therefore attempt to redefine the lifecycle concept and, based on my new definition, take a fresh look at the principles of good management. Although change has been the main thrust of this introductory chapter, one thing always remains constant: Companies that fail to adapt will find themselves in trouble. To put it bluntly: Companies must change or die. This is the understanding that accompanies us as we set out on our journey through the corporate lifecycle.

2.
THE ART OF GUIDING A COMPANY THROUGH ITS LIFECYCLE

2.1 CHANGE OR DIE

Sounds like a typical example of consultant-speak? Consultants are naturally keen to find compelling arguments for the biggest projects possible. Yet there is more to it than that. We can all think of high-profile examples. In Germany, Schlecker is undoubtedly the year's top corporate swan song. But there are also the Neckermanns and the Q-Cells, not to mention Kodak, Saab, Quelle, Hertie, Agfa and Grundig – as well as Kirch and Holzmann, who went to the wall almost exactly ten years ago.

The briefest glance at the history of a few well-known share indices and rankings shows that these cases are by no means exceptions. Change is constant, causing positions to shift and companies to disappear from view or go under completely. This has always happened, and it has done so on a far greater scale than we realize in the course of our day-to-day business.

◆ Of the 100 biggest US companies that constituted the first Forbes 100 in 1917, 61 no longer existed in 1987, just 70 years later. Of the 39 that had survived, only 18 were still on the list.[15]

◆ Of the companies listed as the Fortune 500 in 1970, only two-thirds were still defending their turf in 1993. In the space of just over 20 years, fully one-third had dropped off the list.[16]

◆ Of the 500 companies that made up the Standard & Poor's 500 in 1957, only 57 still figure on the list today. To put it another way, nearly 90% have failed to maintain their standing.

◆ Statistically, a company in the 1920s could expect to stay on the S&P index for 65 years; today, the figure is just ten years.

◆ If ten years doesn't seem very long to you, consider this: The average age of all Western European companies today is just 12.3 years.[17]

Births and deaths – to speak the language of the lifecycle model – are thus business as usual. Change happens. Not somewhere at the back of beyond, but right on our doorstep. A mere 18 of the first DAX 30 companies at its launch in 1988 are still listed on the index.[18] Similarly just 11 of today's 50 MDAX companies have been there since its launch in 1996, 12 of the 30 TecDAX companies (since 2003) and 8 of the original 100 SDAX companies (since 2001).

Not all the companies that drop out of this or that index have disappeared altogether. Some have merged. Others have simply been relegated to a lower division. Many, however, have indeed shuffled off their mortal coil. Recent studies show that roughly 10% of all companies go belly-up every year.[19] That is an alarming figure. So it is perhaps not surprising that entire libraries have been filled with analyses of corporate failure or – to take a more positive angle – ideas about how to prevent it.

The explanations given vary as a function of the period in which they were written and the zeitgeist. On occasion they are also influenced by the consulting concepts that were then in vogue. It is scarcely possible to classify them systematically. Even so, reduced to their common denominator, they ultimately point to three principal reasons for why companies fail.

First: Companies fail because of changes in the market and the environment. Because their products no longer scratch where the market itches. Because their core competencies have become obsolete. Because new legislation has been introduced – in the finance industry, for example, and possibly for auditors too in the future. Because new technology has radically shaken up processes, as the Internet did with retail and the media. Because materials have become too expensive. Or because of a significant shift in factor costs, as in shipbuilding, shoe production, textiles and the steel industry.

It would be easy to add more reasons and examples. The other side of the coin, however, is that not all companies fail. Some do indeed manage to translate change into fresh growth. They do so by making new products or adapting their offerings, improving their marketing, deploying new technology, relocating at the right time and/or globalizing their activities.

Second: Companies are often the cause of their own downfall. Because they (or rather their managers) rest on their laurels. Because they come up with the wrong strategies, are guilty of overconfidence or even arrogance. Because they have the wrong people on board at the wrong time. Because they fail to spot change in time. Because they lack the courage and sometimes the creativity to change swiftly and thoroughly. Because they are unable to break free of inherited ways of thinking. We have already encountered these reasons – in practice, so to speak – in the survey I conducted among Roland Berger's Partners, summarized in Chapter 1. Once again, this confirms our theory: It is not change that leads to failure but the inability to see it in time and respond resolutely.

Third: Companies fail to achieve critical mass or do so too slowly. Let's look at how many companies have managed to defend their position in the various German share indices:

◆ DAX 30: At least 18 out of 30 companies – a good 60% – have managed to stay on the index for close to 25 years.

◆ MDAX: Only 11 of the original 50 companies are still listed on the index today – just 22% over a period of about 15 years.

◆ SDAX: A mere 8 of the original 50 companies are still there. In other words, only 16% have been able to stand their ground for roughly 12 years.

Without reading too much into this simple arithmetic, one trend does suggest itself: Companies that have become big enough to join the DAX have a significantly better chance of not disappearing altogether – a view that, incidentally, is also factored into ratings and credit facilities. Financing almost always becomes more expensive for companies that are demoted from the DAX. Conversely, those firms promoted to the DAX find financing cheaper and easier to come by.

The suspicion that there is a correlation between companies' size and their age is confirmed by a study by Christian Stadler and Philip Wältermann.[20] I have already mentioned that the average age of Western European companies is currently just 12.3 years. That figure should be qualified:

◆ Publicly traded (and hence normally larger) companies have an average age of 28 years.

◆ The average age of companies that post annual sales in excess of USD 5 billion is 48 years.

Size clearly matters. Companies that take the first hurdle, expanding rapidly and becoming "big boys", have a better chance of a longer life. The same principle is also observable at the smaller end of the scale when we look at the embryonic phase of a company's life. The supposed fact that only one out of two startup companies survives the first two years – and that only one in five is still in existence after five years – is the subject of heated debate in many American startup blogs. While proper studies show this failure rate to be greatly exaggerated, the general pattern can indeed be confirmed. A recent study by the Centre for European Economic Research, for example, found that:

- Between 10% and 20% of all startups fail after the first year, between 20% and 40% after the second year and around 50% after five years.
- The probability that a company will fail increases sharply up to the third year after its inception, but decreases again significantly after that.[21]

Incidentally, international comparisons reveal very similar survival rates. Nor has there been any significant change over time.[22] Quite obviously, it is difficult to lead a company to growth (and hence achieve critical mass) and then sustain that growth anywhere in the world. It is an interesting exercise to turn that formulation around, however: Companies do not fail – or, at least, they fail more rarely – if they grow quickly at the start and constantly thereafter.

2.2 THE LIFECYCLE CONCEPT AND ITS HISTORY

Whenever we talk about companies surviving or failing, growing or growing up and having to change, we use examples and terminology from human life. We speak of birth (the inception or launch), puberty (the rapid growth phase), coming of age (when companies mature or reach "middle age") and death (when companies disappear completely).

The idea of describing a company's development in terms of a natural lifecycle is nothing new. As far back as 1914, S. J. Chapman and T. S. Ashton used a similar analogy to nature in their study of the size of companies based on the example of England's textile industry.[23] In the decades that followed, lifecycle concepts became more widespread, initially describing the typical sales curve for products and later as a metaphor for whole industries. Essentially, the concepts used are all very similar:

- Product innovation is the focal issue during the introductory or startup phase: A new product or solution is launched on the market. Average prices are high because of the innovative nature of the product, but then – depending on the intensity of competition – drop off again fairly quickly. Dominant designs and configurations then emerge and an initial transition from product to process innovation becomes apparent.
- The growth phase focuses on quickly ramping up resources, capacity and distribution channels in order to increase market share and realize economies of scale.
- During the maturity phase, growth in demand slows at an increasing rate. Companies that have realized economies of scale can leverage attractive prices to raise their market share and add to their lead.
- In the degeneration phase, products become less clearly differentiated, surplus capacity arises, competition for market share intensifies (causing market share to become more and more expensive) and the product or industry goes into visible decline.

The above description of the various phases makes it clear that more is at stake here than simply the trajectory of sales curves or sales and marketing considerations. Since the volume and speed of sales – i.e. growth – also triggers changes in production and financing, lifecycle concepts remain the cornerstone of many portfolio strategies to this day. The "cash cow" strategy that we know from market growth/market share portfolios, for example, can be explained by the fact that a company, business or product has reached the maturity phase of its lifecycle and therefore only needs to finance slow market growth. However, at the same time it has achieved a substantial market share (usually a market-leading position), allowing it to fully exploit economies of scale and generate cashflows to finance new business.

Borrowing lifecycle concepts and mapping them onto strategic issues seemed the obvious thing to do. The same concepts also found themselves being grafted into organizational and management doctrines[24]: Typical structural and procedural organization patterns likewise change as different phases unfold, as does the style of management, which, again, must align with the varying demands of each phase. The questions that must be asked are self-evident: What constitutes good management in the various phases? Which management skills are of particular importance in which phase? Do a company's values change across the different phases? And are different management personalities needed to optimize management in each phase?

One of the best known lifecycle concepts to examine these issues is that of Danny Miller and Peter Friesen[25], which broadens the familiar four-phase logic into five stages:

1. BIRTH
2. GROWTH
3. MATURITY
4. REVIVAL
5. DECLINE

In his "Leadership Lifecycle" approach, Andrew Ward points to five similar phases[26] and assigns dominant management attributes to each:

1. CREATION (the Creator)
2. GROWTH (the Accelerator)
3. MATURITY (the Sustainer)
4. TURNAROUND (the Transformer)
5. DECLINE (the Terminator)

In our book "Management between Strategy and Finance"[27], Klaus Spreman and I likewise pick up the theme of lifecycles, hence its subtitle: "The Four Seasons of Business". Our primary focus in this work is the constant tug-of-war between management forms dominated alternately by strategic and financial considerations. Even before the financial crisis broke out, our feeling was that the constantly growing power of the capital markets was leading corporate management to focus excessively on financial considerations. Here again, however, the idea of natural lifecycles lent itself as a way to explain our hypothesis. We identified four distinct phases:

◆ Finding and occupying the company's proper position: This phase is all about laying the foundation and developing ideas for future business. It involves becoming convinced of an idea and persuading others too. The focus is thus on strategic considerations and charismatic personalities who know how to win others over.
◆ Building and developing: Ideas now have to take on a more concrete form. Prototypes must be developed and fine-tuned, customer segments identified. All this again necessitates strategic considerations, although these must now be flanked by financial feasibility deliberations. In this phase, the entrepreneur primarily assumes the role of coach and team leader.
◆ Managing growth: The key issue here is to coordinate and plan the conditions to allow the company to scale up. The risks in this phase are particularly high, so risk management takes pride of place and financial considerations gain in importance. The top management acts first and foremost as resource manager.
◆ Harvesting and starting over: Earnings – and hence financial considerations – are top of the bill in this phase. As growth slows, cost calculations can determine success or failure. At the same time, either resources for new businesses must be built up or a healthy exit for the shareholder must be prepared and implemented.

When we wrote the book, back in 2007, the general feeling was that the entrepreneurial world was still in order. In light of the recent crises, however, I would now attach much greater importance to the aspect of strategic management. I would also redraw the lines between the phases in the lifecycle – as I show below.

2.3 A NEW LIFECYCLE CONCEPT

Our fascination with lifecycle concepts is rooted in the fact that they allow us to make forecasts. The assumption is that the life of a product, an industry or a company will unfold in a series of phases. Accordingly, if you know which phase you are in, you can reasonably predict the next phase, the expected developments it will bring and the actions it will necessitate. Which is precisely the point at which I start to worry.

If you know the phases, surely it must be possible to shape them rather than almost inevitably sliding toward death and decay. Companies are not living beings whose death is biologically predestined: They are structures, entities that can be fashioned and molded. Death is not unavoidable. Good management must therefore strive to prevent the company's demise, or to put it to productive use. That is why, in our lifecycle model, Klaus Spreman and I redefined the final phase in particular: The focus is not on dying but on harvesting – on using astute management to reap a rich harvest from the seeds sown in earlier phases.

Staying with this line of thought, I see five reasons why the traditional lifecycle concept needs to be modernized.

First: The familiar charts and figures tend to suggest that the individual phases are all of equal length. Empirically, that is clearly not true. We have already seen that the success of a startup company is decided after three to five years, but that the average age of large companies is 48 years. This alone is an immediate indication that the growth and maturity phases must be many times longer than the startup phase. Logically, therefore, they must also throw out far more opportunities to be seized and risks to be mastered.

Second: The transitions between phases are critical to a company's ability to survive. Can a company translate its business idea into rapid growth soon after its inception, for example? Or can it successfully weather the transition from rapid growth to a more steady upward trajectory? While all concepts accept that these transitions have a part to play, the transitions themselves do not occur at a specific point in time (at best, they can be regarded as mathematical turning points in the lifecycle function). In reality, transitions take place over a period of time that cannot be precisely determined. There are thus powerful arguments to treat these transitions as fully-fledged phases in their own right.

Third: These days, I believe the distinction between a startup phase in which the foundation for a new business is laid "in peace and quiet" and the subsequent growth phase is an artificial one. New technology, fast-paced markets, the danger that different companies in different places might come up with or even copy the same good idea at the same time and the impatience of many financial backers all lead us to one conclusion: The only good idea is one that gets translated into market success and occupies a clear position as quickly as possible. As I see it, this view has already been affirmed by the study by the Centre for European Economic Research mentioned earlier, which suggests that the probability of failure increases up to the third year and then decreases again. As a result, inception and growth have now become so closely intertwined that they should be regarded as one and the same phase.

Fourth: The same goes for the distinctions between growth, maturity and transformation or revival. Conceptually, these distinctions are, of course, highly intuitive:

- During the growth phase, mastering rapid growth is the key issue.
- In the maturity (or saturation) phase, companies must learn to succeed with slower or low growth rates.
- The focus of the transformation phase is to realign the company and gather fresh momentum.

Here again, however, entrepreneurial reality refuses to play ball. The advance of globalization, the emergence of new competitors in Asia, constant shifts in factor cost advantages, new technology, demographic change and, by no means least, the fact that stable economic trends – let alone entire cycles – are scarcely to be found these days[28] all mean that companies are constantly having to adjust and renew or transform themselves. On top of that, our analysis has long shown that only growing companies can enjoy success in the long term.[29] Restructuring must always go hand in hand with growth. Tearing down and building up are two sides of the same coin. Otherwise there will never be any sustainable increase in productivity. Growth and transformation should not be separated: They should form a single phase whose purpose is to realize lasting or constant growth.

Fifth: I have already made clear my opinion that decline, relegation, degeneration or whatever you choose to call the final phase in the lifecycle concept cannot be reconciled with the aims of good management. The objective must surely be to break out of this cycle rather than merely scrape up the crumbs that are left over. We must naturally be realistic in this context too: Markets do contract sharply or disappear altogether. Photographic technology, book selling and mainframes are all examples. These things happen. Core competencies similarly become obsolete or no longer have a suitably dimensioned target market. Other industries find themselves consolidating and are ultimately shaped by nothing but economies of scale and comparative cost advantages. Yet especially in such situations, good management is not about twiddling your thumbs: It is about actively deciding whether and how a restart, a new lifecycle, is possible, or whether it is not in everyone's best interests – those of the owners, yes, but also those of the employees and the company as a whole – to sell the organization in good time and create value in the process.

To what conclusions do these considerations lead us? First, that we need an active understanding of the lifecycle concept. Good management means wanting to break free of a fixed-phase mindset. It means striving to avoid being sucked into a maturity and decline phase, at least in cases where you cannot shape this phase because you are not the scale effect leader. It also means that we should not be looking for the managers that best fit each phase, but for those who are both willing and able to break out of the cycle. And for top managers who will stand behind them. Second, these considerations lead us to conceive of a new, dynamic lifecycle concept and a new definition of the lifecycle phases. This new concept consists of two basic or core phases (Phases 1 and 3) and two transitional or decision phases (Phases 2 and 4). I have given these phases the following names (see figure):

- Phase 1: Occupying a position. This phase is all about getting started, coming up with the right business ideas, developing products and launching them on the market. Above all, however, it is about rapid growth, about going flat out until you have staked your claim and occupied a position that you can defend against competitors.
- Phase 2: Constancy or failure. This phase determines whether structures and processes are good enough to facilitate profitable growth and generate cashflow, whether a company can switch from the fast lane to durable growth at a more modest pace, and whether its potential – in terms of ideas, people, reputation and money – is sufficient to maintain this growth trajectory in the long run.
- Phase 3: Sustainable growth. The third phase focuses on leveraging the potential and capabilities built up in the first two phases and constantly renewing them in such a way that steady growth is possible, that the company can achieve the critical

mass that will give it the chance to stay the course. This phase shows whether the company is serious about continuing to grow, and whether it is prepared to constantly transform and retransform itself in order to deliver on this promise.

◆ Phase 4: Restart or exit. My lifecycle model ends with a fundamental decision and its implementation: Will a completely fresh start in the style of Nokia, Mannesmann and Preussag – i.e. the beginning of a new lifecycle – work or not? The issues at stake here are astute forward thinking, formulating a genuine strategy and having the honesty to see whether an exit or sale might not be the best way to reap a rich harvest.

I regard Phases 1 and 3 as the core phases in the life of a company. Why? Because every example of successful corporate development involves occupying a position: growing a business idea quickly enough to allow it to be defended and then growing sustainably in order to deliver a constant profit stream. Phases 2 and 4 overlap with Phases 1 and 3. For me, they are the critical transitional or decision phases, hence the "or" in their names. These are the times in the life of a company when it becomes apparent whether the management is good enough to anchor steady growth (the transition from Phase 1 to Phase 3) and whether it is ultimately strong enough to make the right, courageous decisions.

Each of these phases obeys its own laws and faces its own challenges. Each could constitute a concept and fill a book in its own right. With regard to our theme of "good management", I see the following points as the most important ones in the individual phases.

PHASE 1: OCCUPYING A POSITION

It is no great revelation to note that you need a compelling idea if you want to start a business. But a startup entrepreneur and his or her team naturally need a lot more up their sleeves than just a good idea. They have to be able to launch and advance the development and design of their product. They have to launch the engineering phase, build prototypes worthy of the name, think ahead to the production and distribution concept, constantly fine-tune the business planning, write market launch briefings, and so on.

THE NEW LIFECYCLE MODEL

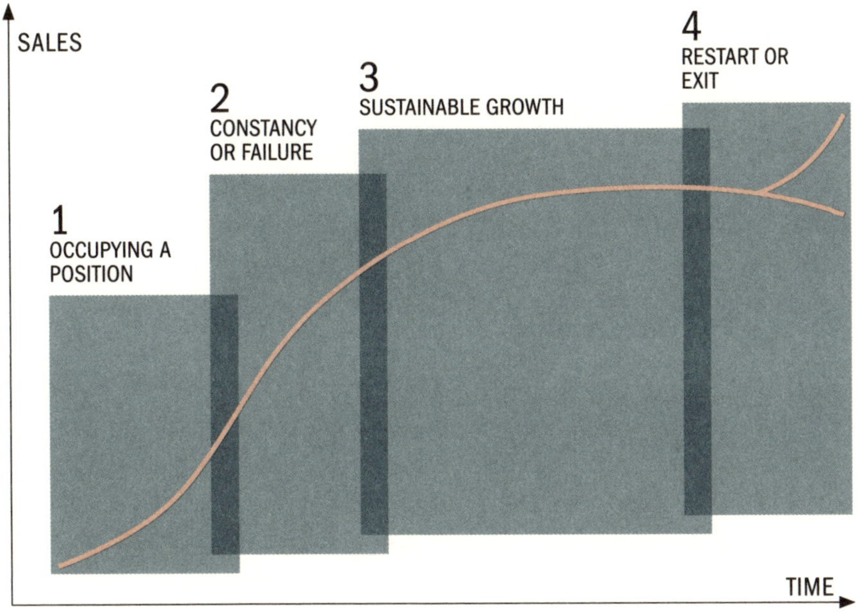

Source: RBSE

Essentially, everything somehow has to get done at the same time. And while that is happening, the fledgling company also has to be stumping up finance, convincing capital backers and other sources of support, looking to build a crack team and the first crop of employees and getting them to buy into the idea too. "Productive chaos" is an apt description. Yet this is also a fascinating, exciting phase – perhaps the most magical in the company's lifecycle. For me, one of the highlights of the year is the annual "Weconomy" event, where Germany's Wissensfabrik ("Knowledge Factory")[30] brings the winners of its startup competition together to spend a weekend gaining advice, discussing problems, kicking the tires of business plans and building networks with experienced top managers. I don't know whether the startup entrepreneurs' expectations are always fulfilled. But for us managers – two of the people interviewed later in this book are part of the regular Weconomy team – it is a wonderful experience to meet them. These newcomers are a source of inspiration, creativity, enthusiasm and optimism.[31]

I get a great deal out of the exceptional mood at these meetings every year. For the startup entrepreneurs themselves, however, the reality can all too often and all too quickly look very different indeed. Maybe the design idea cannot be translated "as is" into a product suitable for volume rollout, or at least not at the budgeted production cost, and compromise becomes necessary. Maybe the engineering phase takes longer than expected and the marketing campaigns accompanying the product launch have to be delayed. Maybe production needs tools that are more expensive than was assumed. Or maybe the funding volume is not enough after all, forcing the startup to try to persuade the banks and capital backers all over again. Above all, the startup team has to keep the faith and run with the business idea.

And even when the company gets off the ground, once the first products are on the market, the work is not over. On the contrary, it now begins in earnest. Sales have to be ramped up as fast as possible in order, as the name of the phase suggests, to occupy a position. This has to be a position that cannot be copied, one that constitutes a unique selling proposition and gives the young company a big enough competitive lead to reach scalability and generate positive cashflow. "Speed to market" is what counts, and that has very practical consequences: More and more orders start pouring in and have to be processed. Invoicing has to work smoothly, as does debt collection. Products have to be optimized and costs constantly adjusted. Structures and processes must be put in place and, just as importantly, lived out systematically.

What does all that mean for good management during this phase? That a startup entrepreneur needs charisma and persuasiveness is as self-evident as the fact that the company founder must be creative enough to have found a really good business idea. That alone is not enough. What is far more crucial is the courage to go ahead and put the idea into practice. Entrepreneurs are by definition people who are enterprising, who want to do something, and that inherently assumes the risk of failure. These days a lack of money is no longer a valid excuse for failing to implement or continue an idea, at least not if the idea has been soundly and professionally thought through. In Germany, for example, there are now so many subsidy and startup programs, low-interest loans and forms of development aid for certain technologies and industries that any and every good idea can find the capital to back it.

Courage – or being courageous, to be precise – is the be all and end all in this entire phase. Courage is first needed to launch a business. More courage is then needed to think big and occupy a position with determination. As long as we are not talking about skilled crafts and small traders, no company these days should think small when it first starts out. Right from the outset, new businesses must be dimensioned to allow for size. Charting this course, and above all sticking to it, can very quickly become too much for one person alone. That is why it is also vital for startup entrepreneurs to quickly build up a close-knit team of colleagues and/or employees who are equally committed to the idea, but who do not necessarily want (or are perhaps not yet able) to stand in the front line. These associates must grow with the business, increasingly shoulder leadership responsibility, and complement and ease the burden on the founder. They must also become mainstays of precisely those values for which the new business stands.

Steve Ballmer, who Bill Gates recruited to Microsoft back in 1980 as employee number 30, is a good example. Another is Susan Wojcicki, who became the first marketing expert to join Google in 1999 and is today regarded as "the most important Googler you've never heard of". A further good example of ideal "teaming" with the founder is Sean Parker, who joined Facebook in 2004 when the company was only five months old and – until a cocaine scandal forced him out – covered Mark Zuckerberg's back as the latter sought to recruit initial investors. Germany, too, naturally has similar examples: the startup team that worked with SAP's Dietmar Hopp and Hasso Plattner; the Leys, who made Escada into something big; Messrs. Jung and von Matt and Messrs. Springer and Jacobi in the advertising industry; and perhaps Theo and Karl Albrecht, the "Aldi brothers".

How do you find this kind of team? Good fortune is undoubtedly part of the equation. But so too is the ability to recognize people's potential, show trust in them and delegate responsibility. And, of course, the ability to persuade people again and again. To start with, you have to convince people of your idea. Then, when things are maybe not going so well and everyone is feeling crushed under the weight of problems, you have to once again show them the potential that is still inherent in the idea.

That is why I believe unalloyed optimism is one of the most important attributes of a startup entrepreneur. To quote Winston Churchill: "A pessimist sees the difficulty in every opportunity; an optimist sees the opportunity in every difficulty." This optimism must be rooted in a profound conviction of the intrinsic value of the idea or business. It doesn't have to be a vision on the scale of a Steve Jobs, who is said to have wanted to change the world from the moment he founded Apple. It is enough to share the ambition of, say, Sam Walton, the founder of Wal-Mart: "Believe in your business more than anybody else!" And, I might add, do so afresh, day after day.

PHASE 2: CONSTANCY OR FAILURE

Let's go back to the basic idea behind this new lifecycle concept. The issue is to quickly transform a new business into a big business, i.e. to occupy a position (Phase 1) and then grow steadily (Phase 3).

In between is my Phase 2, during which it becomes apparent whether the position thus occupied is indeed a dominant one with a future, and whether the company manages the transition from rapid acceleration to systematic, sustainable growth in good time. This change does not take place at a given point in time, but over a period that overlaps to some degree with Phases 1 and 3. This is because it is simply not possible to determine exactly when a position has been occupied to the point where no other competitor might not be faster and better. It is equally difficult to decide when the time has come to take your foot off the gas without giving rivals the chance to fill the void that this potentially creates.

The difficulty – or rather, the challenge – in this phase lies in managing the contradictions. Let me give you just two examples to explain what I mean. Long-term strategic thinking is needed especially in Phase 2 as the issue of how and where sustainable growth can be generated must always be addressed. If it is not, a steady growth trajectory will never materialize. At the same time, however, Andrew Ward is right in saying: "If you don't survive in the short term, there is no long term."[32] Which means that there will always be the need for compromise, and occasionally also for opportunism. Above all, however, the organization must never lose its belief in its original vision.

It is every bit as difficult to manage the second contradiction. The entire organization gets tailored to rapid growth – stepping on the gas, as I put it. If the first phase is successful, what began as a fragile startup becomes a growth machine. However, while this growth mentality must be preserved in order to further consolidate the company's position, it is also important to prepare the structures and processes that will lead to more steady growth.

But growth is addictive. It is a powerful motivator that can easily drive you on to the heady intoxication of new growth record after new growth record. So the problem is: How do you recognize the point when sales targets are becoming unrealistic? And how do you get a sales team that is passionate about raising sales and landing every last order to understand that profit margins are now more important? How, in other words, do you weather the transition from thinking in terms of ever higher growth rates to thinking in terms of market share? How do you teach an organization packed with free-spirited entrepreneurs that risk management systems also have a part to play? How do you prepare an organization for the news that sky-high growth rates are a thing of the past and then still get them to give their all to achieve further growth?

Other challenges naturally also have to be mastered in this phase. Cashflow management is one of them, as rapid growth has to be funded. Not a few companies end up learning the difference between book values and available liquidity the hard way. Personnel management is another challenge, as it is vital to quickly recruit a lot of people without undermining the spirit, culture and vision of the startup phase. It is also important to maintain consistent quality despite rapid growth.

These are all weighty issues that can determine whether or not a company progresses to the next phase of the lifecycle. To my mind, however, the key to good management in this phase is to successfully manage the contradictions I referred to above. They must be managed honestly, not with arrogance, dominance or a know-it-all attitude. And they must be mastered by credible, direct communication: by getting alongside people, by means of careful reflection and by a willingness to take advice and act on it.

Many argue that the founding fathers should, or indeed must, bow out in such transitional phases to avoid threatening the future success of the company.

Because founders are precisely that: founders. Because growth is in their blood. Because they have what it takes to build something out of nothing, but not necessarily to sustain it and take it to the next level. We all know that there are indeed people like that, and every one of us has doubtless experienced situations in which they had to let successful people go – the head of a new branch office or the manager of a new business line, say – because they proved incapable of making the leap to a sustainable growth trajectory. When that happens, hard decisions must be made promptly. That, too, is an element of good management in this phase. Having said that, perhaps it would be better still to ensure early on that startup entrepreneurs' peculiar gift of generating growth is enriched by the complementary skills of other people.

A similar idea is pursued today by some incubators and venture capital firms. These organizations try to match up people who have management skills and would like to become entrepreneurs, but who lack the idea on which to build a business, with others who have a creative idea but lack the management skills and/or experience. Can this arrangement work? Can someone who doesn't birth the idea and therefore lacks the inner passion and total belief in the venture still become a successful entrepreneur? Real-world examples show that, yes, this model can work. I am still uncomfortable with the idea, though. For me, a successful entrepreneur should have both the right idea and the ability to realize it. I don't think it is possible to "believe in your business more than anybody else" if the idea came from somewhere else.

PHASE 3: SUSTAINABLE GROWTH

Let's assume that we have successfully weathered the first two phases. The challenge now is to manage the company in a way that will generate steady growth. Compared to the sprinting in the first two phases, this task is rather like running a marathon. As we saw earlier, it accounts for a far greater share of the company's overall lifecycle.

Why is sustainable growth so important? Because only companies that grow are successful in the long run. Our studies of growth have long shown that steadily growing companies are superior on all counts to average companies[33]: They raise productivity faster, increase free cashflow more quickly (gaining additional strategic leeway in the process), employ more people and create more value for their owners. I see four reasons why growth is an entrepreneurial imperative, outlined below.

First: Traditional business management doctrine identifies the optimum company size as the point at which declining unit costs (due to fixed cost degression and learning curve effects) intersect with the rising transaction costs driven by increasing size (as controlling systems require a more elaborate design, more coordination is needed and additional hierarchic levels are introduced, for example). The logic still applies today, but new technologies now enable transaction costs to increase more slowly. Let me give you a few examples. The cost of data storage today is only 0.00005% of what it was in 1977. The cost of a transatlantic telephone call has declined by 99% since 1977. The number of Internet users has jumped from around 600 million in 2002 to more than 1.5 billion today, opening up entirely new forms of communication and networking. Now, if transaction costs increase ever more slowly, this shifts the optimal company size to the right, making it bigger. And this simply means that companies must grow if they do not want to see their competitive cost position eroded.

Second: If we posit our analysis on the assumption of a well managed company with efficient processes, little room is left for further potential cost reductions. It follows that cashflow can be increased and more value added for the owners only as a result of sales growth. Allow me to digress briefly at this point. I am not advocating a short-term shareholder value philosophy. As I mentioned earlier, Jack Welch was right to point out that shareholder value is a result, not a strategy. And that is precisely the issue here. Any company that has the right offering, looks after its customers and keeps its people motivated and enthusiastic will experience lasting growth and create value.

Third: Globalization and ever fiercer competition are driving prices down, adding noticeably to the pressure on margins in many industries. Food, cars, textiles, furniture, electronic goods and many other sectors are experiencing the same phenomenon. In this environment, a constant sales volume will inevitably lead to dwindling profits. To put it another way: You can only boost your profits by boosting your sales.

Fourth, and perhaps most importantly: Only a growing company is attractive to excellent employees. This is clearly true for consulting firms, who can only credibly offer young professionals attractive career prospects if they are growing. If they do not grow, what is known as leverage – the number of consultants per partner, and hence profitability – deteriorates. But that is true for other companies too. Growth opens up faster career development opportunities, presents more exciting challenges, boosts job security and improves the company's reputation. After all, have you ever heard anyone boast that their company is shrinking?

As intuitive – indeed compelling – as these reasons are, constant growth remains difficult to achieve. Our studies show that only 28% of the 1,700 largest companies in Europe, America and Asia manage to continue growing their sales and profitability for long periods (see figure on page 55). Nearly one-fifth at least manage to raise profitability by downsizing, in other words by discarding unprofitable businesses. In this phase that may indeed be the right strategy, but only if the company succeeds in combining restructuring with growth. If not, it runs a serious risk of becoming one of the one-third of companies that see both sales and profits shrink.

It is actually rather astonishing that so few companies achieve constant growth. The growth imperative is, after all, based on an algorithm that is easy enough to understand: Operational excellence – i.e. good processes, competitive costs and high quality – generates free cashflow that can be invested in growth, leading to economies of scale that in turn improve operational excellence and generate even more free cashflow. And so on, and so forth. The problem lies in the diseconomies of scale that can arise despite falling transaction costs, and for which management failings are almost always to blame. Size corrupts. Companies feel that nothing and no-one can hurt them. They slip into hubris, seeing the future as readily manageable. Top management becomes too distant from the people in the company. The vision becomes diluted. Motivation wanes. Ultimately, nothing really matters to anyone any more.

That is why, in this phase, there are two sides to good management. One is the astute application of the growth algorithms we saw a moment ago: maintaining operational excellence, pressing ahead with innovation, keeping people on their toes and motivating them again and again. The other is seeking to avoid diseconomies of scale. While there is no cure-all here, I do see a number of valid strategies that characterize good management during this phase: decentralized management, fostering a culture of trust and respect, understanding strategy as a project, not waiting for "rule-breaking strategies" and seeing transformation as an ongoing process.

APPLY DECENTRALIZED MANAGEMENT

The world is not flat, as Thomas Friedman claimed, because globalization is being accompanied by stronger regionalization. The BRIC countries have high aspirations and are gaining more than just economic strength. They also want to affirm and strengthen their own culture, identity and geopolitical significance. The consequences are plain to see:

- If the world is becoming ever more multi-faceted, companies need robust local units that are close to the customer. Where customer contact occurs and where deals are struck is also the place where knowledge about trends, needs and market opportunities abounds.
- Where identity and political leadership issues are at stake, a strong entrepreneurial presence in the local and regional market is necessary, if only to make sure the company picks up on the direction economic policy is taking in good time so that it can properly assess the associated opportunities and risks.

Decentralized structures are generally conducive to more creativity. They necessarily admit greater entrepreneurial freedom that nurtures productive competition for the best idea. In principle, the aim is to recreate the climate that prevailed in the first two lifecycle phases: to get people on fire for an idea, wanting to build something and enthusiastic to make their entrepreneurial mark.

FOSTER TRUST AND RESPECT

Decentralized management is possible only where local managers are trusted. Too much control and too many decrees from HQ lead to excessively complex and expensive processes – and almost inevitably to diseconomies of scale. The need,

THE CHALLENGE OF GROWING PROFITABLY

ROLAND BERGER PANEL STUDY OF THE WORLD'S 1,700 BIGGEST COMPANIES [ARITHMETIC MEAN IN % P.A.]

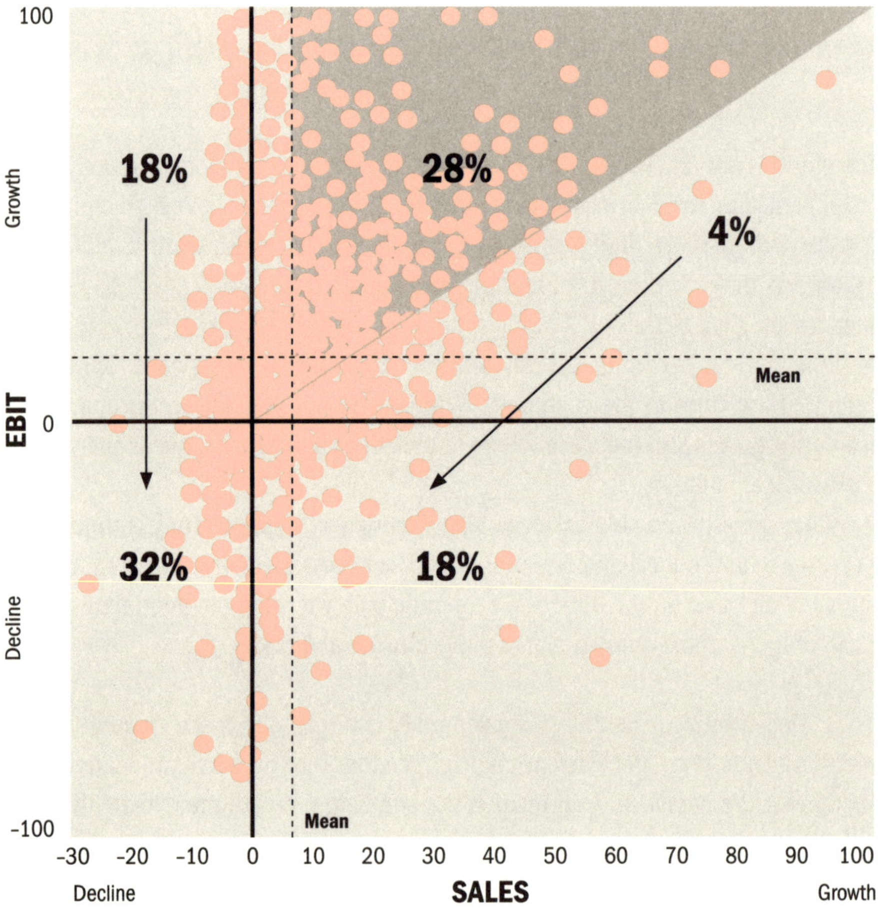

28% of companies have grown profitably since 1991. A further 4% have grown but are in danger of being unable to maintain their profitability long term. 18% of companies have increased their profitability by discarding unprofitable businesses. For 32% of companies, both sales and profits have declined.

Source: Roland Berger Strategy Consultants, annual panel data since 1991

then, is to build the organization upon a foundation of genuine trust (giving individuals the chance to develop their potential) and fault tolerance (giving people a second chance). The organization must also reward good performance and be rooted in respect. It is impossible to lead people responsibly unless you respect them, and respect for one's own task is the best way to avoid overestimating oneself.

UNDERSTAND STRATEGY AS A PROJECT

Corporate headquarters have a tendency to think they are smarter than the rest of the organization. It is no coincidence to discover that "I'm coming from HQ to support you" is one of the three most bare-faced management lies in circulation.[34] For the reasons cited above, this attitude is worse than wrong: It is actually dangerous. Regional political developments can be misread. Market potential can be overestimated or underestimated. Risks can be misjudged. Above all, it is important to remember that the traditional strategy process – first analyze, then formulate a concept, then decide, then implement – no longer works today. Modern companies that want to be quick off the blocks need to closely combine conceptual design with implementation. That is why it is crucial to have as many people in the company as possible involved in strategy development from the earliest stages. People who know why something is necessary may perhaps be more willing to play an active part in shaping change.

One logical consequence of this is that we need to rethink the strategy process and the role played by corporate development departments (or whatever name they happen to go by). In this case, it's not the result – the new strategy – but how you arrive there that matters. Rather than position itself as a know-all detailed strategy developer, corporate development should organize the strategy process, staking out the general framework and using intelligent project management to ensure that as many of the right people as possible get involved.[35]

DON'T WAIT FOR RULE-BREAKING STRATEGIES

Where the need is for steady growth and new growth potential, we are all quick to hope for the one big "rule-breaking strategy": the revolutionary business concept or outstanding product innovation that promises tremendous growth potential. However, experience shows that such major breakthroughs are a rare occurrence.

While the literature on innovation is bursting with suggestions as to how to do it, the few examples they cite never seem to change: Dell, Ikea, H&M and, of course, Apple.

It is dangerous to wait for big breakthroughs when the real challenge lies in steady growth. In my opinion, a better option is for good management to seek to move three key growth levers in two directions at the same time:

- Do not innovate just to gain a technological advantage, but also to improve the productivity of your processes.
- Do not apply marketing strategies merely to set yourself apart, but also to lower the cost of customer acquisition.
- Do not penetrate new markets only to increase sales, but also in an attempt to reduce your factor costs.

In their analysis of "Jahrhundert-Champions" – "champions of the century" or companies that have plied the markets successfully for over a hundred years – Christian Stadler and Philip Wältermann arrive at a very similar set of sound management principles.[36] I find three of their five principles especially important for the sustainable growth phase: efficiency before innovation, learning from mistakes, and the sensitive handling of change.

SEE TRANSFORMATION AS AN ONGOING PROCESS

Efforts at continuous improvement will succeed only if a company stays in perpetual motion. In other words, a constant stream of new change projects must be launched. Continuous improvement must be understood as an obligation, and the enthusiasm of employees must constantly be renewed by fresh and exciting challenges.

This assignment is not dissimilar to the one facing the founder. It demands constant communication and repeated persuasion. Pictures of the future must be painted and repainted. Strategies, structures and even past successes must be called into question again and again. The only difference is that now everything is on a much larger scale – it is effectively open-heart surgery on the living organism.

Above all, good management is about striking the right balance: the balance between pushing your people too far with too many projects and leaving them bored, kicking their heels and slipping into a business-as-usual mentality. On the one hand there is the threat of becoming too heavily focused and limiting entrepreneurial freedom. On the other is the danger of becoming too diffuse and driving complexity. Somewhere in the middle there is a balanced, viable pathway between hasty actions intended to showcase management's force of will and well-thought-through decision paths that can easily become too slow.

PHASE 4: RESTART OR EXIT

Achieving steady growth is a stiff challenge. A simple calculation illustrates the point. Let's take a company that posts annual sales of EUR 50 billion and assume a growth target of 5% per annum. After five years, the company would have to have reached sales of around EUR 64 billion. That is an extra EUR 14 billion, or more than one-fifth the original figure. Annual growth of 7% would produce a figure of EUR 20 billion, and even growth of just 3% per annum would mean an extra EUR 8 billion had to be generated.

This growth has to be generated by new or better customers, products and/ or markets. But it also has to be funded. That is why, over the course of the past decade, many companies have decided to concentrate on their core business and sell off non-core activities in order to free up cash to fuel core growth. RWE and E.On (formerly VEBA) are two good examples: Both diversified widely in the 1990s, moving into telecommunications, environmental services, water and such like, before spinning off these new business activities again in the first decade after 2000. This allowed them to focus both their expertise and their finances fully on power generation and distribution. Aventis has a similar story to tell, having transferred its crop science arm to Bayer so that it could devote its full attention to pharmaceuticals. Similarly, Linde jettisoned its forklift business in order to globalize its core business in industrial gases.

Concentrating on what you do best is a good strategy, except that there comes a point when growth potential in your core business is exhausted. When that happens, three key strategic questions have to be answered:

◆ Is it possible to re-diversify, or expand your diversification? Are there any attractive new business lines that would fit your existing skill sets? And do they harbor sufficient growth potential?
◆ Is the company big enough and strong enough to actively drive consolidation in its core business, acquiring rivals in order to successfully play the endgame in its chosen industry?
◆ Is there a chance of new start, and above all an idea on which to base one? Is there a chance to reinvent the company and start its lifecycle over?

The first question must, of course, be asked on an ongoing basis as early as Phase 3, when the aim is to achieve steady growth. In the "champions of the century" study we touched on a moment ago, Christian Stadler and Philip Wältermann arrive at the same conclusion: The authors assert that one reason why successful companies are successful is because they have diversified into businesses that relate to their own core activities.[37] In the context of the lifecycle concept, this is a finding that I agree with wholeheartedly. If you start diversifying into unrelated lines of business, that has more to do with our third question about a restart. Daimler-Benz during Edzard Reuter's tenure was a good example: The company did not believe it was strong enough to engage in active consolidation (something Jürgen Schrempp later attempted, with just as little success). But nor was it convinced by the future prospects of the automobile market. Accordingly, it targeted major acquisitions in other lines of business in order to reinvent itself as a technology group. However, this example shows just how difficult, dangerous and expensive such a strategy can be. In 1995, the year in which Reuter was replaced, Daimler-Benz announced a loss of DEM 5.7 billion – at the time the biggest loss any German company had ever posted since the Second World War.

Active consolidation – the theme of our second question – can be a smart strategy. Many strategic analyses show that industries tend inexorably toward an "endgame scenario" in which three or four companies dominate, carving up 70% to 80% of the market between them. Jagdish Sheth and Rajendra Sisodia call this "the rule of three".[38] Current examples can be found in the global mining industry (where five companies control more than 50% of the world market), the oil and steel industry, and Germany's retail sector, which is the most heavily concentrated in the world.

If a company cannot actively advance consolidation – because it is not big enough, because its pockets are not deep enough or because others resist its acquisitive overtures – it faces the real challenge of Phase 4: consciously deciding to hit the reset button and start over by reinventing itself, or equally consciously heading for the exit and selling out.

From an entrepreneurial perspective, we would probably all naturally gravitate toward the restart option. Aren't we the creative, successful ones? Don't we have the best people? Aren't we entrepreneurs? Moreover, the good examples are there for all to see:

- Nokia is perhaps the best-known example, having transformed itself from a manufacturer of paper, rubber boots and tires for wheelchairs at the end of the 1980s into the mobile communication industry's front-line pioneer. It was Nokia that first spotted the potential of cell phones as consumer goods.
- Mannesmann is another good example. Well established as a manufacturer of steel, machinery and pipes and affiliated to a domestic shipping company in the 1990s, the German firm transformed itself into a successful and highly profitable telecommunications provider.
- Under the leadership of Michael Frenzel, Preussag too – operating under the name TUI since 2002 – shook off its past as a chemicals, energy, steel and logistics provider and became the world's largest tourism group.
- Another classic example is the venerable Compagnie Générale des Eaux, which divested its traditional core businesses of water and environmental engineering in July 2000, rebranded itself as Vivendi Universal and established itself as France's biggest media group.

This list of positive examples of corporate restarts could naturally be a little longer. I would also put Intel on it: Under Andy Grove, Intel made the leap from memory chips to processors and pulled off a phenomenal branding coup in its chosen industry with the "Intel Inside" claim. IBM is another one, having morphed from hardware seller into a leading provider of software, services and financing solutions. After that we start having to look harder for successful examples. On the other hand, the likes of Daimler (see above) highlight the significant dangers inherent in any restart strategy. To tread this path is to place a heavy bet on the future. For this reason alone, a cogent exit strategy is just as important – and just as demanding in terms of entrepreneurial skills, as it brings with it fundamental change:

◆ Phase 3 focused on an active M&A policy: finding the right targets and snapping them up at the lowest possible price, for example. Now, however, the key issue is identifying the right buyer and selling at the highest possible price.

◆ Up to now it has been vital to keep convincing the internal team, as well as the owners and the capital markets, of the company's innate strengths, its superiority over the competition and its independence as a valuable asset. Now the change of direction must be explained as sensitively and honestly as possible, as well as providing reassurances that the new future will be the better one.

The biggest personal challenge undoubtedly centers around understanding that selling or merging under different leadership at the right time is not tantamount to entrepreneurial failure. On the contrary, it reflects a truly entrepreneurial spirit by reaping the harvest, as I put it earlier. There are good examples of this approach too: the numerous takeovers and mergers in the auditing industry that ultimately produced the dominant "global top four" (PwC, KPMG, E&Y and Deloitte), for example. And then there is VIAG, the Bavarian energy group that was subsumed under E.On. A more topical example is French chemicals group Rhodia, which recently sold itself to Belgium's Solvay. Having joined forces, the two are now the global market leader in specialty chemicals.

For me, however, the most impressive example of a bold exit decision is still that of Hoechst under then-CEO Jürgen Dormann. In 1999, Dormann fought off a barrage of public resistance to enable the long-standing German company to be taken over by France's Rhône-Poulenc, quite simply because he saw no other positive European prospects for Hoechst.

To my mind, Phase 4 is at least as challenging as Phase 1, when the company is founded, or as Phase 3, where steady growth must be achieved. Why? Because in Phase 4, good management means a number of different things:

◆ Having the strategic farsightedness to recognize when the company is entering this phase and making the necessary decisions in good time.

◆ Having the creativity to envisage a "reinvention" and the analytical capabilities to think it through critically and objectively.
◆ Having the entrepreneurial courage to recognize – and communicate – that the reinvention might not work.
◆ Having the negotiating skills and concomitant abilities to conclude the best deal for a successful exit strategy.

That is asking an awful lot and can easily overstretch a company's top management. For this reason, I believe that, especially in this phase, it is important to have a supervisory body that works well. The supervisory board must be quick to spot whether past successes might be seducing the top management team into hubris, whether the team might be stuck in the rut of conventional paradigms, whether it has the creativity, courage and strength for a fresh start or whether it has proposed an exit strategy because this really is in the best entrepreneurial interests of the company, rather than simply the most convenient solution to otherwise insurmountable problems.

In this phase, good management is thus also reflected in good governance, in positive trust and collaboration between the management and the supervisory bodies.[39] That is why I have always advocated a two-tiered board structure that, unlike the Anglo-American system, is posited on the clear separation of these two functions, both organizationally and in terms of who sits on which board. The major advantage is that companies governed in this way have at least a chance that strategies will be considered twice, independently: once by the management board that comes up with them and once by the supervisory board. As complexity continues to increase, and especially given the tremendous uncertainty that prevails in Phase 4, it can only be a good thing if the logic behind a strategy and the decision to restart or get out is analyzed from different angles and on the basis of different experience.

2.4 CONCLUSIONS FOR GOOD MANAGEMENT

Getting back to the title of this chapter, what, then, is the trick in guiding a company successfully through its lifecycle? Let's break that question down into its component parts across the different phases of our new lifecycle model:

◆ How do you get the company to grow quickly but still in a controlled manner in order to create the right conditions for a long lifespan? We have already seen that large companies have a better chance of living successfully to a ripe old age.

◆ How do you manage to escape the (supposedly predestined) maturity phase and instead grow consistently and sustainably? Our analyses have shown that only companies that grow profitably remain successful in the long term.

◆ How do you determine whether a restart and a new lifecycle are possible? And where do you find the courage to chart this course in good time and in such a way that the value of the company is realized before degeneration sets in?

As I see it, our new angle on the lifecycle concept has given us a series of clues, which I would like to condense into three points.

First: In my attempt to factor key principles of good management into the modernization of familiar approaches to the lifecycle theme, I was guided first and foremost by the following considerations:

◆ The traditional lifecycle phase model needs to be rethought as it no longer adequately reflects the conditions under which companies must be managed today. Uncertainty, pronounced volatility and constant trend reversals create an environment in which companies must adjust or transform themselves continuously.

◆ The important thing is to find strategies, structures and management personalities that will help the company break out of the traditional phase model. Contrary to conventional wisdom, companies are not biological entities whose life phases are irrevocably predestined from the moment of conception.

◆ Good management must therefore strive above all to overcome "death" – the final phase in the traditional lifecycle – or at least to put it to productive use, i.e. a use that creates value.

These considerations led me to a new, dynamic lifecycle concept that consists of four phases: occupying a position (Phase 1), achieving constancy or failing (Phase 2), growing sustainably (Phase 3) and effecting a restart or an exit (Phase 4). The essential distinctions between the different phases are as follows:

- Phases 1 and 3 stand for the core phases in the life of a company. Successful corporate development is always rooted in the ability to quickly grow the business to a size that allows it to defend itself, and by its subsequent ability to achieve stable, sustainable growth.
- Phases 2 and 4 are transitional phases, periods in which it becomes apparent whether management is good enough to transform the rapid growth of Phase 1 into more constant expansion and whether it is strong enough ultimately to make the right decisions.

Second: I believe that the new phase model is aligned with the pivotal challenges that we mentioned in the introductory chapter and which face top management today. In surveys conducted by US think tank "The Conference Board", two specific challenges consistently come top: "sustained and steady growth" (see Phases 1 and 3) and "fast execution" (Phases 2 and 4).

This brings us full circle from the general challenges confronting good management today to the specific challenges that each company must master in the course of its lifecycle. If we drill down to the next conceptual level, we thus come significantly closer to answering the questions I posed at the outset:

- A company succeeds in growing quickly if, from the word go, management has the courage and is willing to step on the gas, think big and shoulder risks. "The word 'entrepreneur' means someone who wants to be enterprising," I wrote right at the start. This is precisely the attitude that characterizes the initial phase.
- Controlled growth – weathering the transition from unbridled acceleration to systematic, profitable expansion – can be realized above all when leaders have the ability to manage contradictions: the inherent contradiction between sticking to a long-term vision and leaving room for the short-term opportunism that can keep the company alive; and the contradiction between the urge to grow and to be bold and enterprising on the one hand while at the same time acting on the need to implement structures and processes.

◆ Sustainable growth can be achieved if the company team can be kept in perpetual motion over a prolonged period. Again and again, new initiatives must be launched to kindle fresh enthusiasm and excitement. Strategies and past successes must repeatedly be called into question, even if that seems an annoying chore. At the same time, fresh visions and scenarios of the future must be painted to provide orientation.
◆ The right decisions at the end of the lifecycle are born of the right mix of analytical skills (is the company strong enough for the "rule of three"?), creativity and imagination (what might a restart look like?), and sober realism (would jumping before we are pushed make the most economic sense?). Needless to say, all these skills must be coupled with courage and resilience.

Third: In light of the above, the characteristics of good management can in turn be condensed into three factors that are closely bound up with the art of guiding a company successfully through its lifecycle:
◆ Fortune, which favors the brave
◆ Excellent management skills
◆ The right personal leadership attributes

Good fortune naturally has a part to play. Yet I still hesitate to mention it in this context: It is a little out of the ordinary to label such a vague phenomenon as a success factor. On the other hand, my own personal experience – as well as my close analysis of many lifecycles in preparing this book – shows me that good fortune really is important. For some, it means having the right idea at the right time or meeting people who can support you or your idea at the right time. For others, it means finding a team in which each person complements, appreciates and trusts the others. At the same time, fortune favors the brave, as the saying goes, which at least enables us to give this factor a constructive foundation. So you are more likely to experience good fortune if you are actively seeking opportunities, are open to new possibilities and experiences, and you doggedly back your idea and refuse to become discouraged.

Excellent management skills (or tools, to be more precise) are an indispensable prerequisite for a successful lifecycle. The sure handling of modern planning and decision-making tools is one aspect, of course, but so too is the ability to know the limitations of these tools and to make bold, entrepreneurial decisions. This is true in all phases, but especially in Phase 3, which I see as the most challenging in terms of hands-on management skills. Steady growth can be achieved only if superior operational excellence generates free cashflow that can be plowed back into growth, in order to deliver the economies of scale that enable operational excellence to be further improved. Moreover, this must be done without stumbling into the trap of diseconomies of scale. I know that not everyone will agree with my answer to this challenge, but I am firmly convinced of what I am saying: Decentralization creates entrepreneurial freedom that can lead to better ideas. Trust-based management helps avoid bureaucracy. A strategy process that is understood as a project harnesses diversity and motivates people to press ahead with change.

To me, the right personal leadership attributes are the decisive issue. More than that: I see a number of constants across all four lifecycle phases that stand for precisely those values, convictions and attributes that define good management in the corporate lifecycle. The most important of these are:

- Optimism: This is crucial in the startup phase, because otherwise you don't bother. It has a part to play in the middle of the process too, as no transformation will succeed without it. And it is important at the end, because it gives people a sense of security.
- Courage: Courage is needed at the start to step on the gas, later to slow down somewhat, and at the end to usher in a new lifecycle by pressing ahead with active consolidation or drawing up an exit strategy.
- Keeping your balance: A healthy balance is needed between conviction and reality in the launch phase, between growth and efficiency in "middle age" and between ambition and reality at the end of the lifecycle.
- Trust: Trust in oneself is vital at the outset, then in the team, and then in the organization and the people who constitute it.
- Fairness: The same rules must apply for everyone, so there must be no special dispensations for the founder at the start and no hubris at the end of the corporate lifecycle.
- Integrity: This is needed in order, by sheer force of personality, to manage the conflicts and contradictions that can occur as the different phases unfold –

contradictions between short-term and long-term benefits, between values and the occasional need for opportunism, between what is possible and what is realistic.

As I see it, this list also shows that it is wrong to seek managers who are best suited to a given phase. The company will fare best in all phases with managers who live out these values and attributes.

Is it really that simple? Can successful lifecycles really be put down to good fortune, certain skills and, above all, specific management attributes? The interviews with experienced and successful top managers in the next chapter will, I hope, show whether my conceptual deliberations hold water – and where they perhaps need to be corrected, extended or adjusted.

3. "HOW DO YOU MANAGE?"

INTERVIEWS WITH ENTREPRENEURS AND BUSINESS LEADERS

3.1
ABOUT OUR INTERVIEWEES

A book like this is designed to appeal to established business leaders, up-and-coming managers and the interested public. If it is going to feature interviews on the subject of good management, it has to choose the interviewees very carefully. We used the following criteria:

◆ The managers interviewed must verifiably have set management standards over an extended period.

◆ Their achievements must set an example in the eyes of employees and external observers alike.

◆ They must be willing to reveal something of their personality to help us understand what makes successful company leaders tick.

Alexander Rittweger, the youngest of our four interviewees, runs Loyalty Partner GmbH. The Payback bonus system that Rittweger founded under the company's holding structure in 1998 has proven to be one of the most successful company launches in Germany in recent years. He has experienced he "growing pains" of a startup and has shown how they can be dealt with in order to bring business success into a steady state.

Once that works, sustainable growth is possible. And to make sure it does work, company leaders must not only align their organizations with ongoing change, but must play a part in actively shaping that change. Two managers who have done so very successfully, with a manifestly keen eye and sensitive touch, are Franz Fehrenbach, until recently Chief Executive Officer and now Chairman of the Supervisory Board at Robert Bosch GmbH, one of the world's biggest automotive suppliers, and Dr. Jürgen Hambrecht, former Chief Executive Officer of global leading chemical company BASF SE and now member of the supervisory boards of several large German companies.

Another individual who has had a formative influence on the German business community is Professor Wolfgang Reitzle, who realized a ten-fold increase in the value of industrial gas producer Linde AG while safeguarding the company's independence. The changes at Linde are a classic example of how a company leader can fundamentally restructure a corporate group and create lasting value in the process.

As different as the four interviews are, they all confirm one thing: The demands placed on good management remain the same throughout a company's lifecycle process, even though they are lived out differently by each manager in each specific situation. Before proceeding to the interviews, let us briefly get to know who we are talking to.

ALEXANDER RITTWEGER

Alexander Rittweger, born 1965, studied Business Administration in Passau and Mannheim. He began his career at management consulting firm Roland Berger in 1992, where he advised clients such as Lufthansa on strategy and sales issues. The successful frequent flyer program Miles & More inspired him to design the cross-industry customer loyalty program known today as Payback. In collaboration with Lufthansa and Roland Berger, he thus founded Loyalty Partner GmbH and set up the Payback system in 1998. In fall 2012, the Payback partner network included 30 retail and service companies and 500 online shops. In Germany alone, more than 20 million households use Payback cards. Another 30 million have joined them in Poland, India and Mexico. Rittweger has been pressing ahead with the internationalization of the bonus system since 2009. At the end of 2010, US financial group American Express acquired a majority stake in Loyalty Partner GmbH for nearly EUR 500 million. The seller was a British financial investor that had bought its shares from Lufthansa and Metro in 2005. Founder Alexander Rittweger stayed on as boss and himself still owns 20% of Loyalty Partner. In fall 2012 the company employed 750 people, of whom 300 work in Germany.

FRANZ FEHRENBACH

Franz Fehrenbach, born 1949, studied Industrial Engineering in Karlsruhe and joined Stuttgart-based Robert Bosch GmbH in 1975. After holding a series of management posts, he was appointed Executive Vice President Finance and Administration in 1996 and, a year later, President of the Diesel Systems Division. In 1999, he became a member of the group's Board of Management, which he chaired from 2003. Franz Fehrenbach drove the development of eco-friendly products that help conserve natural resources, while also overseeing international expansion, especially in Asia. When he took the helm at Bosch, the company was posting annual sales of EUR 36.4 billion, of which 71% was earned outside Germany, and net income of EUR 1.1 billion. In the year in which he stepped down from leading the company, Bosch reported record sales of EUR 51.5 billion, of which 77% was earned outside Germany, and net income totaling EUR 1.8 billion. On Fehrenbach's watch, the number of employees rose to over 300,000 around the globe. Since July 2012 he has chaired the Supervisory Board and remains Managing Partner at Robert Bosch Industrietreuhand KG. He also sits on the Board of VDA, the Association of the German Automobile Industry, is a member of the Board of Stifterverband für die Deutsche Wissenschaft ("Association of Sponsors for the German Science Community") and a member of the Supervisory Board at BASF SE. Franz Fehrenbach has won repeated awards for his commitment to promoting sustainable management and entrepreneurial responsibility.

DR. JÜRGEN HAMBRECHT

Dr. Jürgen Hambrecht, born 1946, studied Chemistry in Tübingen and earned a doctorate in Organic Chemistry. His career began in polymer research at chemical group BASF in Ludwigshafen in 1976. Hambrecht moved on to operational management assignments as of 1985, overseeing the company's East Asian business, for example, from 1995 through 1999 from a base in Hong Kong. He was appointed to the Board of Executive Directors of BASF SE in 1997 and became its Chairman in 2003. His overriding goal was to safeguard BASF's independence and grow it into the world's leading chemical group. To this end, he sold non-core businesses and ramped up the group's special chemicals activities, in some cases by means of major acquisitions. In 2011, the year he stepped down as Chairman of the Board, BASF had 111,000 people on its payroll, posted sales of EUR 73.5 billion and reported net income of EUR 6.6 billion, the latter two figures breaking company records. Today, Jürgen Hambrecht is a member of the supervisory boards of Daimler and Lufthansa and Chairman of the Supervisory Board at Fuchs Petrolub. He is also a member of Germany's Ethics Committee for a Safe Power Supply and devotes his time to "Wissensfabrik – Unternehmen für Deutschland e. V.", a "knowledge factory" that seeks to get children excited about science.

PROFESSOR WOLFGANG REITZLE

Professor Wolfgang Reitzle, born 1949, studied Mechanical Engineering and Industrial and Economic Science in Munich. He joined BMW as a production specialist in 1976, very quickly taking on various management positions in development before becoming the member of the Executive Board responsible for research and development in 1987. In this capacity, he was instrumental in shaping the success that the automaker continues to enjoy today. In 1999, during BMW's takeover of Britain's car manufacturer Rover, of which he was critical, Reitzle moved to Ford Motor Company as CEO and Chairman of the Premier Automotive Group. The year 2002 brought a switch to the Executive Board of Linde, where he was appointed CEO in January 2003. In the space of four years, Reitzle transformed Linde from a plodding conglomerate into a highly profitable and sharply focused gas and plant engineering company. In 2002, Linde's more than 50,000 employees generated sales totaling EUR 8.7 billion and net income of EUR 240 million. For 2012, analysts expect sales of around EUR 15 billion and net income of EUR 1.3 billion. Wolfgang Reitzle also serves as Chairman of the Supervisory Board of Continental AG, is a member of the Administrative Board of Holcim and an honorary professor at the Technical University of Munich's Faculty of Economics.

"WHEN PEOPLE KNOW THERE IS SOMEONE WHO WILL HELP THEM TO ADVANCE, POWER FLOWS TO THAT PERSON ON AN INFORMAL LEVEL."

ALEXANDER RITTWEGER

3.2 ALEXANDER RITTWEGER ON COMPANY FOUNDERS AND THEIR PERSONALITIES

MARIO MÜLLER-DOFEL: Mr. Rittweger, you were 33 when you launched Payback in 1998. Today, it is the biggest customer loyalty program for retail and service companies in Germany. How did the people around you react to your plan at the time?
ALEXANDER RITTWEGER: Most sounded pretty skeptical. I think many friends and acquaintances just assumed that I wouldn't go ahead with what I'd announced. My father was utterly appalled – he couldn't understand my decision at all.

What bothered him?
The fact that I was trading the relative security of being an employed management consultant for the risk of starting a company. He knew how I was getting on at Roland Berger, especially as I'd already been chosen as a Partner. But other life experiences too had given me a completely different risk profile. I simply wanted to know whether I could do it.

Did other people's skeptical reactions worry you?
No. I knew what I was doing and I had a strong partner in Lufthansa. My consulting activities there had given me a thorough knowledge of the Miles & More system, and I was convinced that I would be able to map this successful system onto a retail context.

What would you have done if you had failed?
I didn't have a plan B. I just didn't think about failure, although it was by no means unlikely.

Back then, you were the youngest Partner at Roland Berger. They had a lot of trust in you. Wasn't it rather an ungracious exit?
It was nothing of the kind. I value loyalty, but a company isn't a monastery! And I didn't defect to the competition. I left the company to live my entrepreneurial dream. Quite apart from which, the company has done splendidly without me...

How did your then boss react?
Roland Berger? He was cool about it. He understood me and even backed me with venture capital. That was naturally fantastic for me and ultimately profitable for him, fortunately.

Are you a gambling man?
Not at all. Although I have a positive attitude toward risk, I see myself as a very controlled person. I always hold on tight to what I have before embarking on new adventures.

How did you enlist then Lufthansa chief Jürgen Weber's support as another venture capital backer?
As a consultant at Roland Berger, I spent six years helping Lufthansa, during which time I often worked directly for Jürgen Weber. He trusted me to successfully implement the Payback idea and contributed DEM 10 million.

What was the risk for you?
Above all, there was the risk of losing my reputation if I made mistakes. Anyone who burns the millions thrown at him by Jürgen Weber and Roland Berger is likely to become very well known in the German economy, but is less likely to get back on their feet very quickly. On top of that I had also invested all my own money.

Apart from venture capital and a good business plan, what does a company founder need in order to be successful?
[Thinks carefully] Inner strength, very good judgment, decisiveness, sufficient ambition to set lofty targets and, to quote from a book about the outstanding strength of leadership shown by polar researcher Ernest Shackleton, who died in 1922: It is not enough to have a strong will or be a model of extreme endurance. It takes the ability to generate enthusiasm to make a great leader.

You read books about leadership to prepare for the Payback challenge?
For heaven's sake, I really had other things to do at the time. We worked like crazy! I read the book about Shackleton years after the company was launched. It made a deep impression on me.

Why?
Shackleton became famous for his Antarctic expedition on the Endurance, on which he set sail with 55 men in 1914. They wanted to reach the South Pole, but never got there because their ship was crushed by ice masses in November 1915. Far from civilization, it seemed like that was the end of the story. But for two years, Shackleton led his men through the ice and back home, without losing a single one of them.

What do you most like about Shackleton?
He was a modern leader who built teams with complementary skills, who took on an incredible, extremely risky challenge and who, while pursuing it, always gave top priority to the life and safety of his people. He personally always went on ahead.

How big was your team when you set sail to conquer the retail world with Payback?
In the beginning there was just me and the telephone. Then I looked for 15 others with whom I could get through the first two years until Payback went to market.

Signing up with a small firm that is not even generating any sales yet is not everyone's cup of tea.
I first used headhunters to try to find good, experienced people. But those people normally already work in attractive positions and don't want to join a startup with all the risks that that entails. So I opted for inexperienced enthusiasm with a good educational background. Apart from myself, everyone on the initial team was under 30.

Established corporations also have plenty of demand for inexperienced enthusiasm with a good educational background. How did you convince your first employees about the Payback idea?
In a similar way to Shackleton. He placed an ad that read: "Men wanted for hazardous journey, small wages, bitter cold, long months of complete darkness, constant danger, safe return doubtful, honor and recognition in case of success." People who respond to that kind of pitch were the ones I was looking for.

There are applicants who promise more than they can deliver. How did you avoid those people?
Fortunately, I only made a few mistakes. But naturally I also learned from my mistakes when we started. Later, I set up a personnel department. And when I interview an applicant in person, I normally ask them mostly unusual questions to bring them out of their shell. Generally that is when I see what kind of a person is sitting in front of me.

You need certain types of people for certain tasks. How did you deploy your initial employees?
First and foremost, I made sure that their attributes would have a corrective effect on me. When you're the boss – be it in the startup phase or later on in the lifecycle – you always need intelligent opposition if you want to stay on track.

Did your initial team have one strength that you still remember vividly?

Yes: They could put up with huge frustrations. However hard the setbacks were, we always got back on our feet again.

When, for example?

Before we got started in Germany in 2000, we had acquired retail partners to participate in the bonus program based on a commitment by Deutsche Telekom. Telekom was a powerful draw, especially as their stock market valuation was going up by a couple of billion a month. They were effectively the darling among Germany's major corporations. Three months before our market launch, however, I went to a meeting at Telekom's head office in Bonn and was told: We think your program is great but it's going to have to be called T-Payback, not just Payback. The logo should be magenta instead of blue, and we want a 51% stake. I resisted the temptation to accept what was a simple solution, but to my mind a bad one. I broke off the negotiations, flew home and went out with my closest associates to an Italian restaurant. We drank a lot of red wine and devised a plan for how we could keep the other partners on board.

What did you do?

With tremendous energy, enthusiasm and the right facts, we managed to convince our partners that Payback would still work even without Deutsche Telekom. For four weeks I raced around Germany like a man possessed, talked a lot, negotiated a lot and didn't sleep much. A little later, in March 2000, we did indeed get off the blocks – and had a million customers in just four weeks. It was incredible!

Was this "rescue job" your first big test as a company boss?

Yes, this and another, similar situation. Another tremendously important company had also committed to becoming a Payback partner. But suddenly their chief negotiator made it clear to me in a meeting that he wanted to dominate Payback. Once again, I packed my bag and left. After that, the chief negotiator softened and accepted a partnership of equals. As far as my leadership role was concerned, it was important for my people to see that Rittweger takes a clear line and is predictable, even when the going gets tough. He does things we maybe wouldn't dare to do – and they work. That is how you earn trust.

When did you realize that Payback could one day be as big as it is today: 50 million end consumers as customers in four countries, 20 million of them in Germany alone?
The German figures are roughly the same as the ones I had in my old business plan. International growth, which only began in 2009, is far more difficult to forecast. But once you've persuaded a country's big consumer companies to sign up, it follows the same pattern everywhere.

Was the transition to steady growth smooth or were there problems?
We naturally had to introduce new structures, and we had that under control. What was more difficult was that the glory of our initial successes made us tend to be a little arrogant.

How did that manifest itself?
In negotiations with a number of potential partners, for example, we were focusing above all on our own goals instead of being truly customer-oriented. When potential partners who first wanted to wait for us to get going saw the benefits that Payback would yield for them, we hardly had to do anything to actively sell the bonus program. Incidentally, selling starts for me when the customer says no. And some of us felt like we were the biggest kids on the block.

How did you notice?
To give an example: One of our people asked whether we should even bother responding to the interest expressed by a retailer who was the number three in Germany in its segment. Things like that cost us

money and, for a time, tarnished our reputation. Fortunately, they did not cost us our survival as a company.

How did you get the team's feet back on the ground?
We got rid of a number of staff and got back to our old way of doing things.

What management conflict was the most difficult to deal with in your team in the early years?
There was no one major conflict. But there were lots of niggling little growing pains that we dealt with constructively in just about every case. As a result, only one member of the current management team has not yet been with us for over seven years.

How did your management role change when you guided Payback into the steady growth phase?
From my perspective, the bigger the company grew, the more the employees saw me as an institution. They were no longer as free and easy with me as they used to be. Instead, they kept a careful distance and looked up to me.

Many company bosses enjoy such a status. Do you?
No, because I like being a normal human being.

Have you changed as a company manager over the 14 years since you launched Payback?
Above all, I have achieved a better balance. That helps me deal better with shortcomings.

Would you tell us one of them?
I always try to base everything – including my own performance – on the theoretical optimum. In practice, however, that optimum can hardly ever be reached. In the past, I often couldn't keep a lid on the frustration that that caused me.

Meaning...?
In my communication and management behavior, I was often too negative. I criticized too harshly and gave too little praise. I think that has improved now.

How did your staff react to overly harsh criticism?
A kind of solidarity grew up among those who took the criticism. They closed ranks and stonewalled me, so to speak. The aim was to make sure I only heard things that would not elicit criticism. That kind of behavior can very quickly filter down to the lowest level of the hierarchy. Having said that, I know our business very well – I built it, after all – so I still see a lot of what isn't working properly without the need for detailed analyses. However, the bigger the company gets, the more difficult it becomes even for insiders who have the clearest visibility to pick up all the details. By this point at the latest, overly harsh criticism and stonewalling can do a lot of damage.

What corrective action did you take?
When the initial battle for survival has been weathered and a steady state has been achieved at the very latest – which was after about five years in our case – the founder and boss has to implement different structures and delegate responsibility. That is the time when you have to relax a little and trust your people.

How can employees build a career under your leadership?
By observing attentively what happens in our company, by acting courageously and focusing on the real issues rather than acting out of a political or power-hungry motivation. By only making promises they can keep to colleagues and customers, and by having the courage to tackle problems even in the face of resistance.

And if people do not fit in with this culture?
Then it may be that, for all their outstanding skills and competencies, the organism rejects them like a foreign body.

Going back to delegating responsibility: Many company founders have a very hard time doing precisely that.
I have to admit that I was the same. But I did manage to let go. In 2008, I relinquished the business management of Payback Germany and have since concentrated on strategic tasks.

And how are you coping with a life devoid of operational engagement?
[Laughs] Let me put it this way: I devote myself to the things that I really enjoy doing and that I do well. Since the start of 2012, I have gone back to taking charge of our product innovation and am also overseeing the internationalization of Payback, alongside my holding assignments. I believe that, in doing so, I have found my place in the organization.

Why do you believe you are good in these two areas?
My feel for product design usually dovetails with the findings of consumer surveys. I find that I can rely on my gut feeling. And for new Payback partners abroad, it is me, the founder of the company, who is the one who can sell our product with the greatest credibility and enthusiasm.

Would it be better to let a different management personality take over in each lifecycle phase?
Not if the boss is able to adapt the company's structures and his or her management behavior to each different lifecycle phase. Processes like that demand a lot of careful reflection and close insight. Many company founders and employed executives in Germany demonstrate how they can work and run their companies successfully.

Were there times when you felt you were losing control of the running of Payback?
Yes, in 2010. Back then, our majority owner, British financial investor Palamon Capital Partners, told me that they wanted to get rid of all

their shares. Just five years earlier, Palamon had bought Lufthansa's and Metro's shares in Payback and so acquired a majority interest. At the time, Palamon had promised to hold its shares for more than ten years and support our international expansion. But now the company wanted to cash in big time as early as 2010 and to milk Payback. I stood up to them, whereupon the Palamon management said: Okay, you've got until the end of the year to sell Payback for EUR 500 million. If you don't, you're out.

Where did the EUR 500 million figure come from?
That was a 50% mark-up on the stock price of our biggest competitor.

You could have said that was not feasible and waved goodbye...
I founded this company, I put my heart into it! Apart from which, 20% of the company belongs to me. If I had just cleared my desk and taken my hat, I would have had to stand by and watch while Palamon put my entrepreneurial achievement and my assets at risk. I knew what they were planning to do.

What happened next?
I allowed myself to be forced into the selling process and told every potential buyer: "We can talk about everything but the price. I need EUR 500 million by December 15, otherwise you don't get the company." Then, finally, there was a solution: US financial group American Express paid the requisite fee and we were back in good hands.

To whom do institutional tools of control such as Payback's HR and controlling departments report?
They report straight to New York City, to the headquarters of American Express.

Does that undermine your leadership position in Germany?
No, it doesn't. First, we are good partners. And second, I make sure that attractive product innovations, ongoing internationalization and good numbers continue to give us a solid basis for collaboration. Power can derive from being an authority on the subject matter, which is much more healthy. When people know there is someone who will help them to advance, power flows to that person on an informal level.

Many entrepreneurs look back on the startup phase as the best time in their professional career. How do you rate it so far?
The startup phase was very definitely the most intensive phase, and it brought with it truly magical moments. But I also really like the phase we are in today. Because now I am seeing the seed I sowed in Germany years ago begin to bear fruit internationally.

"MANAGERS WHO COME FROM AN AUTHORITARIAN BACKGROUND CAN GET A CULTURE SHOCK HERE."

FRANZ FEHRENBACH

3.3 FRANZ FEHRENBACH ON BEING BOLD AND TRUSTING OTHERS

MARIO MÜLLER-DOFEL: Mr. Fehrenbach, the introduction to this book asserts that "the world is changing at an ever more rapid pace. 'Truths' that had become flesh and blood are suddenly unmasked as error". What springs to mind when you hear these words?
FRANZ FEHRENBACH: I think first of the fundamental error of believing you can always foresee political and economic developments. Bosch always used to stick closely to its planning, preparing very detailed business plans for a three-year period. Then the financial crisis in 2008/2009 showed how quickly such plans can be worth less than the paper they're printed on. Now we've just got a strategic ten-year plan, which focuses primarily on technological developments.

Have you made any changes to your business planning?
We believe that long, stable phases of growth are a thing of the past. We must prepare ourselves for very volatile times ahead. Accordingly, the Bosch management now prescribes far less detailed planning targets and has also shortened its planning horizon. The focus is now on scenario planning and enabling the company to respond swiftly and flexibly.

Has that also forced you to change your management style?
Not fundamentally. But I have intensified internal communication. If a company is to become more agile, more flexible and faster, then the top management must be able to reach and engage in dialog with executives and employees more quickly.

Isn't that the job of direct superiors in the individual units?
In the past, that might have been enough. But today I believe that company leaders have to get a lot closer to their people, right down to the lowest level of the hierarchy. And there are good tools – such as social media channels – that let you do that nowadays.

Has running a company become more complex?
Back when I began my studies in the early 1970s, people were already saying that the world and the economy are growing ever more complex. That's true. But we also now have better means at our disposal to master this complexity.

So on balance, running a company has not become more complex?
Let's say that, more than ever before, mastering complexity – by simplifying processes, raising productivity and developing the organization – has become the most important task for company chiefs. That's especially true when you need to establish steady growth in a volatile environment.

This book also claims that change must be dynamic, but handled sensitively. What do you understand by that?
For example that employees can have their say before decisions are made, and that they can thus see themselves as shaping the process of change. That is hugely motivating and improves people's acceptance of change. Additionally, managers must always be respectful in the way they communicate.

How do you communicate in a respectful way?
Let me give you an example. When I took over as Chairman of the Board of Management at Bosch on July 1, 2003, the first thing I did was to send an e-mail to every employee worldwide, outlining the values and objectives that we share and the importance of the part that everyone in the organization plays. Many of them thought that the mail had been wrongly addressed and wasn't really intended for them…

What was so unbelievable about it?
Bosch had never seen such a mail, although it was all the better received as a result. It can sometimes be so easy to express respect. Today, it has become normal for our management to use blogs to engage in ongoing dialog with our people. That sort of thing is really appreciated.

When you took office, you saw your principal challenge as being "to strike a balance between economic, ecological and social concerns." That is a weighty statement – especially given that, at the time, a mood of doom and gloom prevailed in the economy, the DAX had plunged to 3,000 points and the Iraq war had just broken out. Why didn't you just promise to "drive by sight", like many company bosses do in times of crisis?
"Driving by sight" was what people were talking about during the 2008/2009 crisis. Personally, I don't like the phrase, because it means adopting a short-term focus. Especially during a crisis, we need to be looking at the long term and staking out the key tenets of our strategy. When we at Bosch realized in 2008 that we could forget our numbers-based planning, we switched to management by principles instead.

Which means?
That absolute top priority goes to the long term. One example is that we didn't stop a single one of our important research and development projects in order to reduce the loss of EUR 1.2 billion we posted in 2009. And this course was charted in full agreement with the shareholders.

Did you prefer to save on personnel?
The management and the employee council promised each other that the burden of the crisis would be shared fairly across everyone's shoulders. And that's exactly what, later on, everyone felt happened. Incidentally, that was another of the principles by which we ran the company.

Company bosses often tend to interpret the word "fair" in a different way to employee councils.
We only had a single interest group. From the top management to our people in the factories, we were all in the same boat. Everyone knew what "fair" meant without anyone having to negotiate or put it down in writing. We issued no detailed savings targets, but executives and

employees all pulled in the same direction. For the first time, we even refrained from switching to central control, although that is customary in crisis situations.

Centralization involves prescribing every detail from the top down. Why is the practice so widespread, especially given that difficult times can also be overcome with decentralized management?
Psychology plays tricks on many bosses. They feel compelled to take personal control of everything. Yet even in a medium-sized company, the boss never has everything under control. During the financial crisis, we gave our people a great deal of entrepreneurial freedom. Being entrusted with greater responsibility was an extremely powerful motivator. That was one reason why Bosch weathered the crisis so well and so quickly.

What do you consider the most important difference between central and decentralized management styles?
In a decentralized structure, the company leader has even less control over individual activities than in a centralized organization, so trust is crucial. You have to work hard to establish that trust – you don't get it at the push of a button.

How much time does a company boss have to earn the necessary trust?
The best thing is to create a culture of trust years before you switch to a decentralized organization. Many companies fail to do so and then wonder why they run into difficulties.

Many managers scarcely have any trust in others because they are afraid their trust might be exploited. Where do you find the courage to trust?
[Thinks] I was the youngest child at home and had to work on my parents' farm and in the vineyard from an early age. But they also gave me a lot of care and support, and the people close to me never let me

down. I also learned to perform as part of an organism, first in the family, then as class representative in every school class, and later as captain of a successful handball team. Still later, I experienced the same trust and support within my own family, first and foremost from my wife. All this experience has taught me how important it is to treat people as equals and to respect them.

You once said: "To trust also means to be bold. If you want to get something done, you need courage – courage for the future." How do you stimulate such courage at Bosch?
That's a very difficult question...

What do you mean?
On the one hand, we challenge our people to be courageous in what they think and do. Many do indeed take bold steps. On the other hand, we often react the wrong way if things don't work out. Courage has a lot to do with taking risks.

How do you mean, you "often react the wrong way"?
If someone takes a manageable risk and something goes wrong, managers are often quick to express their displeasure at the failure, saying things like "Why didn't you think of this or that?"

Do you do that too?
Yes, sadly, I do that too from time to time.

The boss is always wiser after the event, isn't he?
[Laughs] As are the employees concerned. We should criticize them less, and instead encourage them to keep on going. I think it's often less a lack of courage on the part of employees that puts the brake on companies' dynamism and more the wrong reactions from management when things go wrong. That's something we're working on.

"Sales and profit growth" rank among the words used most often by company managers. As if the world revolved around that alone, scoff the critics of capitalism. Can you imagine more important things?
In his last will and testament, Robert Bosch charged his successor to energetically develop the company and keep it financially independent. For us, "energetic" means a sales growth target of 8% per annum and pre-tax profits of 7% to 8% of sales. However, it's very important to realize that, while profitable growth is a necessary condition for a successful company, it's not enough on its own. That's why focusing on the future takes precedence over focusing on profits at Bosch – always with a view to preserving long-term financial independence. Having said that, a company can only survive if its environment survives as well. In the long run, profits and growth won't work without an awareness of the environment.

Which brings us back to the balance between economic, social and ecological concerns that you advocate. Is there any role model who you look up to?
Robert Bosch, of course. He stood for a healthy balance of economic and social responsibility.

"Red Bosch"...
He was called that because he was the first boss to introduce the eight-hour day and free Saturdays.

A benevolent corporate manager?
That he was. But he also had an eagle eye for the economic benefits. He discovered that people's performance peaks in eight-hour shifts. If shifts go on for longer – which was commonplace in his day – quality and efficiency problems begin to pile up. So he introduced the eight-hour day, albeit in two shifts which, at the same time, allowed him to make far better use of his operating resources. In my time as Bosch chief, I have placed greater emphasis on ecological values in addition to economic and social responsibility.

"Green Franz"...
That's what people sometimes call me, by analogy to "red Bosch".

Are you proud of that nickname?
Yes, because sustainability is a critical topic, and will remain so in the future. And because Bosch makes a whole series of energy-efficient and resource-saving products.

The relevance of social values in the company has long been the subject of heated debate in Germany. What importance does Bosch attach to these values?
I immersed myself in this issue as far back as the 1990s. Maybe that was one of the reasons why I was appointed Chairman of the Board of Management in 2003. Back then, we had already launched various initiatives to draw up a canon of values and a mission statement. I then condensed these into what we called our "House of Orientation", which consists of our vision, values, mission statement, core competencies and the Bosch business system.

Isn't the value of such formulations, which are often rather abstract, generally overestimated?
On the contrary. The House of Orientation is the key to our strategy. It is the foundation for our 300,000 employees and for our international expansion.

Why for international expansion?
On my watch, 75,000 new employees have been added to Bosch, some of them through acquisitions and many of them abroad. Compared to Germany, our foreign operations have fewer managers who have been fed our culture from their earliest days and who constantly communicate it. So the House of Orientation is all the more important for them.

Is that something you think or something you know?
It's something I know. We have conducted employee surveys every two years since the mid-2000s, with a response rate of nearly 90%. Some 80% of respondents say that they are proud to work for Bosch. That's an unusually high level of identification and loyalty, that has a lot to do with awareness of our values.

In its 126-year history, Bosch has experienced highly dynamic development that has brought constant change. How has the company remained so agile?
Let me take an example from recent history. In the early 1990s, many German companies introduced the kaizen methods – continuous improvement processes (CIP) – that came from Japan. Yet the initial wave of euphoria passed almost completely in a very short time. Bosch, however, is still practicing CIP to this day. As far back as the 1920s, Robert Bosch challenged every employee to strive to improve the status quo. That is CIP in its purest form.

But how does it work? Most people don't really want change.
That is why the management must convincingly explain the need for change. On this point, I like to quote the philosopher Odo Marquard: "The future needs the past." And I would add: "The past needs the future." Without it, the company would disappear at some point. Change is just as important as continuity.

Change is often generated by a fresh wind from the outside, through new managers who come from other companies. Yet you have been with Bosch since 1975, and most of the other Bosch managers have been there for a long time too. How is it that, specifically at Bosch, staff continuity has ensured dynamic change and growth?
The "helicopter" management style that some people practice – floating in, kicking up a lot of dust and then flying off to face the next so-called challenge – is completely incompatible with our management culture. Our stated aim is to guide our own junior managers to the

top. They get the chance to work in 150 countries, gather experience in a wide variety of product areas and shift between different business lines. Ideally, given so many development stages, talented individuals won't even think about wanting to leave the company.

Have you never attempted to recruit external applicants for senior management positions?
Of course we have. But it turned out that we have a very distinctive management culture, and a lot of people have problems with that if they join us late or at too high a level.

Despite the focus of your values?
Maybe because of it. We nurture a collaborative management style and a certain culture of consensus right up to top management level. In other words, we would rather spend a long time hammering out a solution to which everyone can then give their backing. So someone who comes from a very authoritarian culture where the boss reigns over everything, right down to the "bottom", can get quite a culture shock at Bosch.

What exactly can trigger such a culture shock?
Our employees refuse to follow a manager who doesn't involve them sufficiently. An organization like that can wield plenty of power and let you run into a brick wall. We prefer to bring in fresh wind from the outside at the middle management level, where new people have more time to become attuned to our unique culture and grow into higher-level assignments.

How would you describe the kind of people that apply for Bosch management positions?
Since our management style is well known, we mostly get applications from people who set little store by personal vanities. Nor do people who are motivated by hefty bonuses come to us – fortunately, because that reduces our risk levels. A number of financial institutions have shown how the prospect of huge bonuses can ruin entire organizations.

Managers sometimes use other people's mistakes to expose them as losers. How do you deal with that kind of thing?
To me it is a clear-cut case: Playing the power game must be absolutely taboo. In the Bosch management team, we decide things together, so no one can be blamed as the loser after the event. We stand by each other even when failure happens.

You are known for your habit of communicating aggressively even when setbacks occur. Why do you do that? Before you took over as boss, that wasn't common practice at Bosch.
In recent years, I have done a lot to make Bosch more open not only on the inside, but also toward the outside world. Dealing openly with setbacks is a particularly good way to earn credibility and trust, even in our relationships with customers. My best leads emerged during difficult times, because we always act on the principle that we stand by our word.

That sounds a little simplistic.
Obviously it's a painful process in many cases.

Can you tell us about any of the painful experiences?
I remember what we called the "valve crisis" in our diesel injection pumps, which arose soon after I took office. The small valves we sourced from one of our suppliers didn't work, and that supplier had sourced the surface treatment from one of its suppliers. We couldn't tell Audi, BMW and Daimler how long it would take for us to get to the bottom of the problem and deliver pumps that would work. So I told them: "I don't know." At first, I really didn't know how we were going to get out of this one. Those were dreadful days and nights for me and my colleagues.

So there was something you didn't have under control and you admitted that you didn't know the solution? Brave, but risky…
One customer immediately sent two of their best material specialists to help us. That was fantastic. We worked on the problem together

and that created a bond between us. All the customers who were affected stood by us. In the final analysis, it always pays to be honest in business.

Mr. Fehrenbach, wouldn't you have liked to stay on a little longer as Bosch chief?
No, nine years is enough. Somebody younger should now call the tune and lead the company into its next successful phase. Changing the boss after ten years at the most is conducive to maintaining the dynamism that is vital to survival.

"ERRORS OF SELF-PERCEPTION ARE A COMMON REASON WHY COMPANIES AND MANAGERS FAIL."

DR. JÜRGEN HAMBRECHT

3.4 JÜRGEN HAMBRECHT ON THE RATIONAL AND THE EMOTIONAL

MARIO MÜLLER-DOFEL: Dr. Hambrecht, the world has for years been changing so fast and so profoundly that economic forecasts no longer provide companies with a reliable planning framework. How can a company boss still draw up long-term strategies?
JÜRGEN HAMBRECHT: Company leaders need a telescope to track social, technological and regulatory developments. And they need a microscope to see what their company is currently able to achieve and what it will need to achieve in the future in light of these developments. They must also be prepared to say exactly what their company's position is, with ruthless, no-holds-barred honesty. Having weighed up all these insights, they need to define a development corridor bounded by best-case and worst-case scenarios. Suitable strategies, which should be as flexible as possible, can then be developed on this basis.

Are any typical mistakes made in this process?
Many managers deceive themselves, especially when describing their company's position.

What exactly do you mean?
They believe their company to be the number one when in reality it is only the number three, for example. Or they believe that they are still a niche provider when their products have long since been commodities. As a result, they overestimate their pricing power, underestimate the pressure to innovate, and communicate unrealistic goals, which in turn frustrates employees. Errors of self-perception are a common reason why companies and managers fail.

On what basis did you develop your long-term strategy as CEO of BASF?
When I took office in May 2003, the Board of Executive Directors mapped out our corporate guidelines. These specified what BASF is, what the company does, how we act, where we want to go and what we expect of our managers.

And what do you expect of your managers?
The top management committed itself to ensuring clarity and realism, encouraging enthusiasm and inspiration, demonstrating strategic and operational leadership and setting an example in terms of performance and speed. We allowed ourselves to be measured against the yardstick of the underlying details.

You forgot the sales and profit targets.
No. Sales and profit targets are not mentioned in the guidelines. First and foremost, we committed to a mindset that is based on values. Everything else, including sales and earnings growth, derives from that. The only quantitative target was that we want to earn a premium on our cost of capital. For many years, neither the chemical industry in general nor BASF had managed to do that.

And then?
Most of the targets that we set ourselves within the framework of our Vision 2015 were reached before I stood down as CEO in 2011, despite all the crises over the past decade.

You once said that growth is not per se a target worth striving for. What, then, would you see as a target worth striving for per se?
Managing on the basis of values that promote the economy and human wellbeing. Every employee needs to understand that ecological, economic and social issues are at stake – in other words, sustainability.

Speaking of social issues: More and more people complain of being overstretched in their job, while some say that they are not stretched enough. How can managers strike a healthy balance?
Through social skills. By that, I primarily mean getting close to the employees. Managers need to identify the strengths and weaknesses of their team members, the context in which they live, how they see the world and what problems and potential they have. To do so, it is imperative to talk to each other openly and often.

And if employees don't want to open up to their managers?
Then basic trust is lacking. That is deadly and therefore needs to be called into question. Managers are responsible for actively soliciting information in communication contexts. But employees are responsible for providing it too, so that both sides know and understand each other's expectations. If bosses don't know what the people in their charge expect, it will be almost impossible to deploy and motivate them properly.

More and more employees suffer from burnout. What do you see as the causes?
In my experience, the majority of people affected have exaggerated expectations of themselves. They demand more of themselves than their skills and abilities can deliver, and then they despair because they fail to live up to their own expectations. On top of that, there is often tremendous pressure from the outside. Many people then project their fears onto managers within the company.

So the managers are not to blame?
Managers can be a cause too, if they lack empathy. But managers are not automatically to blame when employees are not doing well.

Aren't you making things a little too easy for yourself?
On the contrary. Managers are the ones who have to try to solve these problems in order to build the best team. That takes team spirit,

motivation, appreciation, expectation management and dialog in an atmosphere of trust. All of which means that managers need to be able to look critically at themselves, which, sadly, we sometimes see too little of.

What does appreciation mean to you?
It means respecting everyone and showing it. It can be seen in small gestures, like extending your hand in welcome, addressing employees by name, looking them in the eye when you talk to them, pouring coffee for them. The supposedly small things can do a lot of good. Managers also need sufficient empathy to try to sense what's going on with their people. I also believe that it's very important to be authentic. I am my own man: I say what I think and I do what I say. I lived out these principles, first formulated by Alfred Herrhausen, and I urged the entire BASF team to take them to heart too.

So why are there still so many communication problems?
To my mind, that's because we don't talk to each other enough. That also has to do with the Internet and new media.

How do you mean?
The e-mail culture is a really big problem. It diminishes the personal element and cultivates distance. You're constantly deluged with unimportant information. Important trains of thought are continually being derailed. The more we are inundated with information, the less we think!

How do you deal with that?
I take the liberty of communicating very little by e-mail. Some start the morning by working through their e-mails for an hour. Not me. To overstate the case slightly, I am not available on-line.

Are you not afraid of missing something?
No. I get the really important information anyway. And I don't need the unimportant stuff. I need the peace and quiet to think about things

creatively. I detest the idea of consuming instead of thinking. If you become increasingly addicted to every little bit of information, you lose track without really gaining any fresh insights.

So the best way to reach you is by phone?
I treat my cell phone the same way as my e-mail account. I switch it on when I need it, but I refuse to be permanently available.

So how were you available to your people when you were the head of BASF?
Face to face! In the corridor, in the canteen, in the office. People know that my door is always open – which it still is to this day, incidentally. If I can talk to someone and look them in the eye while doing so, I know whether my words are getting through. It is when we stop meeting personally that management problems start to pile up.

Does that mean you even avoid videoconferences?
That depends on how present I have to be. If you want to persuade someone, you have to know what's going on in the room. That means you need to see the body language of the person you're talking to. I remember when we acquired our US rival Engelhardt in 2006. It started out as a friendly takeover. For "day one" – the day when the acquisition took legal effect – our communication experts prepared a speech for me. When I met with the people in the US, however, I realized I wasn't getting across to the managers I was addressing. So I pushed the manuscript aside and extemporized. And I believe it was a huge success. In a videoconference, I'm sure I wouldn't have picked up on the mood.

While you were at the helm, BASF bought and successfully integrated many of its competitors. How did you prevent the cultural struggles that one usually encounters?
Integration is the highest art in acquisitions. It is critical to success. For me, day one always laid the cornerstone for successful integration.

On day one, I would meet up with all the managers of the company we had acquired, at ten in the morning at their headquarters.

What did you talk about at those meetings?
About our strategy and our vision. What do we want to achieve with the company we have taken over? What has it been doing well, and what does it have to do better within the BASF family? What does that mean for the employees? How many employees will be staying on board and how many will have to leave the company to allow us to leverage the necessary synergies? I would tell them: "I don't yet know the details of how we will do it, but we will do it together with you. You are now BASF employees, and you're worth just as much to us as people who've spent their whole career with us." That is why an acquisition always involves changes for the workforce at the parent company too. The meetings always ended with an open discussion involving all the managers from around the world.

For how long did you visibly help with the integration process?
After day one, I retired into the background and left the operational side of integration to a specially appointed integration manager, whose job was to implement plans ratified by the Board of Executive Directors.

BASF has a predominantly decentralized organization. What advantages do you see in this type of organization over central management?
The individual units are closer to the market and generate more innovation. The structures are more complex, but they are also faster and – given the relatively high degree of responsibility they bear – provide employees with greater motivation.

How important is trust?
Trust is the basis for every business transaction, be it in a decentralized or a central management structure. Responsibility is delegated on the basis of trust. If you don't trust this division of labor, you have

a problem. If you don't delegate, you have to do everything yourself. No one can do that, and it puts an end to good teamwork.

What place do org charts have within the company?
They show the structures and processes by which staff are organized, and the limits of their responsibilities.

Are they a tool to convey a sense of security?
On the surface, maybe. In reality, however, things often work differently to what you see on the org chart, because work teams organize themselves. Security is conveyed by teams' personal dealings with each other and their trust in the management. Org charts shouldn't seduce us into thinking in terms of boxes and templates.

When company bosses tell lies in order to create a sense of security, that is a dangerous tightrope walk. Do you believe that there is justification for "white lies" if they have a positive effect?
For how long can a lie have a positive impact? When will the truth come out? Is that really the way to solve problems? No, I'm not going to stand up in front of people and tell them lies. I have to tell them the unpleasant things too, even if that unleashes a storm.

Top managers normally use analysis and lots of charts and numbers to substantiate their strategies and vision. Entrepreneurial skills hardly seem to get a look in. Have analytical tools made gut feelings superfluous in the operational business context?
By no means. Analysis is useful to help prepare decisions and explain them later on, but good management demands a good nose for business.

What part does a good nose for business play for you?
My head and my heart – my mind and my emotions – are always involved in the decisions I make. The mind takes care of the hard, rational analysis. Once that is done, I listen to what my heart is

saying. If something is wrong, the question arises: Why do I have such a funny feeling about it? That's when the wealth of experience gained over many years makes itself felt, in your gut, and those feelings shouldn't be ignored. In the end, though, you have to make a decision, and that's something I've always enjoyed doing. Weak decision makers often end up analyzing themselves to death.

Has your intuition ever led you astray?
Rarely.

When, for example?
Many years ago, I wanted to set up a production base for a certain polymer in China. Economies of scale were needed if this was to be done profitably, and that was only possible in collaboration with partners. I knew a Japanese firm whose technologies complemented those of BASF. The firm's boss, whom I knew well, was open to such an approach. To be able to build the factory in China right away, we also needed a Chinese partner. I preferred to have someone from my network with whom we had worked very well together. I brought the two sides together, we agreed on the basics and my intuition told me: This thing is going to work. Then the other two suddenly got cold feet.

What was wrong?
I had underestimated the emotional and cultural barrier, as well as the mistrust between the Japanese and the Chinese, something that is rooted in history. I had also overestimated the collaboration between the top managers. My attempts to mediate were of no use.

Getting back from intuition to "hard, rational analysis": When capital market analysts want to assess business strategies, the first thing they demand is numbers, on a quarterly basis. Doesn't that tempt managers to adopt a quarterly mindset?

I think too much has been read into the "quarterly mindset". Most companies simply cannot be managed on such a short-term basis. At BASF, for example, it takes around five years from planning a production facility to opening it. And it can take as long as 15 years from product idea to market readiness. The Board has no option but to think for the long term.

So the obligation of providing quarterly reports must be rather annoying?
No. I simply accept that there are different interests. The company leader's job is to create value in the long run. But analysts have to recommend shares to their clients or advise them against them on a daily basis. They need up-to-date justification for their recommendations, which is what they find in our quarterly figures. That has positive aspects for companies.

Which are?
We know how the outside world sees us. There are a handful of analysts who are excellently informed about BASF and the chemical industry, for example. So when one of them tells us: "Some of your margins are worse than those of your competitors. Why is that?", that can be useful for us internally. Employees are often more willing to believe criticism from the outside than when the boss says: "We are not good enough."

Company bosses have a poor public image. People think that they make too much money and have lost contact with the man on the shop floor. How can you rebuild trust?
Such generalizations are wrong. The vast majority of company leaders, who conduct themselves in an exemplary manner, all get tarred with the same brush. In most cases, the company's own people are very happy with their management, by the way. At BASF, the figure is over 80%. However, once a reputation has been destroyed, it's very difficult to restore it. That's why we and the Wittenberg Center for

Global Ethics together launched an initiative for responsible action in the business community. More than 60 companies have signed up to the initiative already.

What do you aim to achieve with this initiative?
We must sharpen the focus on good management, starting in the earliest stages of child education, in schools and with the public at large. If we engage in many individual actions and prove that we are promoting human wellbeing in a responsible way, the image of managers will improve again over time.

How do you share your principles of good management in the supervisory boards you sit on?
By only becoming a member of supervisory boards to which I can contribute some additional benefit. At Daimler, for example, that includes my knowledge of integrated value chains and my experience of Asia and Russia. And I contribute my thinking about values to all the companies I work with, because I am convinced that value can only be created if you uphold values.

"ONE ASPECT
OF GOOD
MANAGEMENT
IS NOT
SURROUNDING
YOURSELF WITH
OPPORTUNISTS."

PROF. DR.-ING. WOLFGANG REITZLE

3.5 WOLFGANG REITZLE ON LEARNING AND TEACHING

MARIO MÜLLER-DOFEL: Professor Reitzle, you said in fall 2012 that you were preparing yourself for "permanent uncertainty". Has anything ever been certain for a company leader?

WOLFGANG REITZLE: A company boss seldom finds ideal conditions, and that is what makes it exciting. But the current debt and financial crisis is a genuine watershed. It shows that the unbridled availability of cheap money has led to excessive and unsustainable growth. On top of that, investors have become much more critical in their choice of investments. Over the next ten years we will probably see relatively low economic growth coupled with pronounced volatility. The resultant uncertainties don't exactly make it any easier to run a company with a view to the long term.

What, specifically, has become more difficult?

When companies want to grow through acquisitions, for example, they have to be very fast these days. When you get up in the morning, the world can already look different to when you went to bed. The markets have become very nervous and short-lived. It's easy to be caught on the wrong foot even in the middle of a transaction.

So does caution now prevail in the Linde boardroom?

Watchfulness is closer to the mark. If you only ever act cautiously, you can't develop a company. You've got to try to harness volatility for your own ends.

How do you do that?

When the value of companies fluctuates significantly, opportunities arise for attractively priced acquisitions. But the right timing has become more crucial than ever.

What else can companies do to minimize the risks inherent in the global economy?

They can establish as stable a footing as possible. Smart diversification can play a part. I no longer unreservedly accept the credo, repeated by many company leaders, analysts and investors, that a company focused on a single business line is inherently superior to a more broadly-based company.

What arguments do you have against this view?

An intelligently diversified company is better placed to cushion external risks and has more chances to grow than a firm with a one-sided focus. Our acquisition of US homecare company Lincare, completed in summer 2012, is a good example. Lincare is an excellent complement to our existing activities. At a stroke, it gives us a leading role in the North American healthcare market, in which we have only operated as a component supplier up to now.

How is integration progressing?

Very well. But you can't compare it with the takeover we did in 2006.

Back then, you acquired the British company BOC, one of Linde's rivals in the industrial gases business.

That's right. Unlike BOC, however, Lincare operates in the US in a business in which Linde has not been present up to now. So in this case integration is less complex. The company has first-class processes and will essentially continue as is for the time being.

Let's look at Linde's success story right from the beginning. Before you were appointed CEO in 2003, you were first a member of the Executive Board at BMW and then at Ford Motor Company – an alien background to Linde's home industry. Yet management experts advise companies to fill top jobs with internal candidates. How do you see this issue?

In principle I would agree, although here again there is no generally valid rule. Ultimately, when you're choosing a new boss, you always have to take into account the specific situation of the company.

When does an external candidate make more sense?
In particular in situations where a company has failed to groom its own managerial talent for the top job. Or when a company has to be restructured to survive but there is no suitable internal candidate.

Don't potential top managers learn how restructuring works back at business school?
Theory and practice are still two completely different things. Even if you do have internal managers who master the art of restructuring, that doesn't tell you whether they would actually go ahead and break up the structures they themselves have built, for example.

What might prevent them from doing so?
Doing so is an admission that their previous strategy has failed. That's not nice for anyone. That is why some managers prefer to ignore their mistakes rather than correct them, even if that attitude can do a great deal of damage.

Hans Meinhardt, the former Chairman of the Supervisory Board at Linde, is quoted as saying: "Wolfgang Reitzle is not a nice boss." Was that because you don't like people who see things through rose-tinted glasses?
I think what he meant was that it isn't comfortable to have me as a boss.

Why do you believe that?
A company boss can't focus on keeping people comfortable. I wasn't like that then and I'm not like that now. In addition, when I became CEO at Linde, the Supervisory Board may have had different expectations about what I would do for the company.

What expectations?
I was supposed to develop and grow Linde, albeit giving top priority to the forklift and refrigeration divisions. So when I said I wanted to get rid of both and build up our industrial gases business instead, not everyone saw that as good news. It meant a completely new start for Linde.

And the Supervisory Board simply swallowed your plans?
I obviously had to convince them first – which didn't take long.

How did you do it?
We took an X-ray of where Linde was at – a detailed and brutally honest analysis. The results clearly showed that the group would do better if it realigned itself.

In what areas, for example?
Apart from its fundamental business strategy? In its human resources activities, for example. Or in IT, where we lacked stable, robust structures. Linde had a lot of catching up to do in these areas.

Let's go back to the opportunities afforded by adverse circumstances. Were there any in this case?
Yes, there were. Because of the shortcomings in the company, I had more room to act than I had suspected. And then there was our absurdly low stock market valuation: EUR 2.7 billion at the time when I took office. That was not even EUR 23 per Linde share! Since then we have increased our market capitalization nearly tenfold.

Was that the primary objective of your work?
Well, for starters, the low valuation at the time made sure that absolutely everyone knew where we stood as a company. Linde was an acquisition target. To avoid being taken over, it was imperative for us to increase the value of the company.

A magazine article about you in 2004 said: "At Linde, Reitzle has to bring a 60 year-old corporate culture into the 21st century, which demands tremendous managerial strength."
Would you go along with that?
I would perhaps have put it like this: The corporate culture had to become more international. It was also important to significantly improve the performance of the company as a whole. All managers and executives had to play a part in that.

Were they able to meet your demands, just like that?
Not all of them, obviously. As of a certain level in the hierarchy, we did have some churn. Not everyone was willing to accept the necessary culture change. Some felt that they were not up to the new requirements.

You don't have a guilty conscience?
No, because a company's ability to survive in the future has to take precedence over personal interests. And that cannot only be true for the chief executive.

What does "corporate culture" mean under your leadership?
Back then, it was about establishing a positive, sports-like climate of performance in the group, including a willingness on the part of every individual to constantly improve. That attitude still shapes what we do today.

As far back as 2003, the world's industrial gases business was already dominated by just a handful of corporations. In 2006, Linde swallowed its much larger British rival BOC in a hostile takeover. Weren't you afraid that Linde might have bitten off more than it could chew?
The financing volume was indeed twice our market capitalization at the time. Under similar circumstances, that kind of transaction would scarcely be possible today. By the way, the only way to contain the fear of overstretching yourself is to think through every conceivable

negative scenario on a rational basis and draw up a solution for every eventuality. Ultimately, though, it takes resolute courage to take such a big step, because a measure of risk always remains.

What was the mood like at Linde ahead of the impending BOC deal?
Hardly anyone knew anything about it. Discretion commands absolute top priority on such matters. If news of our intention had leaked out into the public domain, BOC's shares would have shot up and we could have forgotten about buying it. A major acquisition has nothing to do with democratic discussions.

And when it did become public knowledge? Didn't the people at Linde think that their boss had gone crazy?
Possibly. But if they did, nobody told me [laughs]. I believe a lot of them were proud, really.

And those who weren't proud?
They understandably took a different view of the takeover, because they already suspected that we would sell the forklift division to finance the deal.

In the 1990s, you were on the Board at BMW when that company's acquisition of British automaker Rover resulted in a EUR 5 billion loss. Was that experience useful to you when you took over BOC?
Certainly. I learned what you need to pay particularly close attention to and what pitfalls to avoid.

What things do you have to pay close attention to?
The most important thing in a takeover is that the transaction must make strategic sense. In the case of BMW and Rover, this fundamental condition was met only to a very limited extent. The drawbacks of the acquisition had been addressed, but not everyone wanted to see the risks…

Do rational arguments sometimes get pushed aside even in company boardrooms?
Sadly, there are times when reservations, however justified they may be, are misread as personal criticism. In a business context, that can cause billions to be destroyed on occasion. With a very small team, we examined every aspect of the Linde/BOC transaction systematically and came to an unambiguous conclusion: This takeover would add value. Which is what ultimately happened.

Would you please explain in a little more detail why this kind of deal and other investments are sometimes doomed to failure from the word go?
It gets difficult when a company boss doesn't think an important decision through clearly and carefully, but is instead lead primarily by emotions. When he then shows his hand to the supervisory board, the capital markets and the general public…

… he can still pull out if necessary?
In theory, yes. In practice, that's unlikely, because people are often afraid that pulling out will be interpreted as weakness. That's why some managers develop tunnel vision and lose their way.

Theoretically, other board members and the supervisory board should provide corrective input.
Theoretically. But if one member of the board actually does speak up to correct the path on which the boss has already set his heart, the others often just stand by and wait and see what will happen. In the worst case, they keep their misgivings to themselves and, to be on the safe side, give their backing to the chief. One aspect of good management, however, is not surrounding yourself with opportunists.

Once a takeover has been completed, how do you have to manage to prevent a "war of the cultures" between the new partners?
Let me take the example of Linde and BOC, again. After the acquisition, we behaved differently from how many BOC employees expected. We didn't come in like know-it-alls and start laying down the law.

How did you behave, then?
When mapping out the new organizational structure, for instance, we adopted an integration-based approach right from the start. We used a transparent selection process to fill functions solely on the basis of qualification for the job. No one was given preferential treatment because of their company background. In this way, two people from BOC were appointed to the Executive Board at our newly organized company. That won us a lot of points, especially in the UK. And that too helped us to conclude the integration faster than we had planned.

Turning to the exits: You sold refrigeration and forklifts – two of what had once been Linde's core activities – in 2004 and 2006. What criteria did the "right" buyer have to satisfy for you?
What was crucial then is still crucial now: Based on the customary calculation methods, the right buyer had to pay a fair price for the company, provide evidence of solid financing and credibly demonstrate its ability to lead the company to lasting success. How else are you supposed to persuade an employee council to vote for a sale?

Why is the employee council important?
Because any such far-reaching decision has to have the backing of the workforce too. If you try to force it through at all costs and against the will of the employees, that will harm both the buyer and the seller and will erode value. Looking back at the disposal of the forklift division, I am still pleased that, at the critical meeting of the Supervisory Board, both the capital backers and the representatives of the workforce voted unanimously in favor of the sale.

How did you manage that?

You can only do that by engaging in trusting collaboration with the employee council over many years, and by involving them in the decision-making process early on. It also helps if the employee council has an entrepreneurial mindset. At the time, I gave our employee council a detailed explanation of the risks that would exist if Linde was taken over and broken up into its constituent parts. We explained the fundamental reorientation of the group and presented them with a reliable buyer.

Can you still say the same today?

Absolutely. The US investors Goldman Sachs and KKR have proven themselves to be highly professional, forward-looking and fair owners. I still enjoy good contact with the head of the employee council for the forklift division, and with his deputy.

You haven't always aligned your management style to such an extent with representatives of the workforce. In 1999, the employees' representatives on the BMW Supervisory Board prevented you from becoming the boss of the Munich-based automaker.

It's true that I didn't have a particularly good relationship with the employee councils back then. In my capacity as product engineer and member of the Board responsible for development, I didn't see nurturing such relationships as one of my most important tasks. And it's only natural that the cost-cutting plans that I had for Rover ran into resistance on the part of the employee councils and the workforce. Today, I have learned that a company boss needs the support of the employee council if he wants to do a good job of running the company. In that sense, I learned some useful lessons from this experience.

4. THE MARK OF GOOD MANAGEMENT

4.1 BOTTOM LINE: WHAT REALLY MATTERS

"I can't say whether things will be better when they change. But one thing I can say: They have got to change if they are to get better." In my opinion, this witty aphorism by Georg Christoph Lichtenberg very aptly summarizes the findings of my discussion of good management. So, what exactly has to change? And above all, how will things get better?

Let us briefly recapitulate the individual steps in our analysis and the conclusions we have arrived at:

- We began with the premise that uncertainty is increasing as people are no longer sure what is going on: because the world is changing ever faster; because it isn't flat, but is growing ever more rich in diversity; because ever greater leaps are being made in technology; because risks are increasing; and because markets are becoming more volatile.
- One consequence of this is that business "truths" that have become flesh and blood can suddenly turn out to be errors. If it is no longer possible to paint a realistic picture of future developments, then it also makes little sense to calculate a detailed strategic plan for the next ten years or to base investment decisions primarily on quantitative computations.
- Incidentally, this is not to say that we have to kiss goodbye to our business strategy and planning tools. What it does mean is that we must learn exactly what the limitations of our models and methods are, and critically examine the outcomes they deliver.
- My conclusion from the above points was that good management must once again become more enterprising, because the ability to calculate and predict everything is waning. It is important to say clearly what you are about, paint your own picture of the future and not go running after every new trend. What matters is the ability to reflect critically upon developments and show a willingness to cultivate an interdisciplinary mindset if political and social developments are to be factored into business decisions.
- I linked this conclusion to what I see as some good news: Corporate management is once again becoming more direct, more personal, more entrepreneurial. It

can no longer hide behind models, concepts and techniques. On the contrary, it demands personality, courage, the ability to think and reflect, and a system of proven values. Managers need convictions; they must nail their colors to the mast.

◆ This understanding is especially important to me because it reflects an important challenge to good management: that of communicating a sense of security to the people in our companies. In the past, this was fairly easy to do by presenting clear strategies and numbers: "That is our goal, this is how we are tackling the problems." Today, however, it is not possible to be so unambiguous. Instead, today's leaders must be able to overcome uncertainty on the strength of their personality and values.

◆ The importance of personality and behavior is underscored by our analysis of why companies fail. They do so primarily because they (or rather their managers) rest on their laurels, become too self-confident and arrogant, lack the courage and sometimes the creativity to change swiftly and thoroughly, and are unable to break free of inherited ways of thinking.

◆ This observation is also specifically confirmed by my survey of my colleagues, the Partners at Roland Berger. As a rule, companies do not fail because their managers have no command of the operational tools of the trade. On the contrary: In functional terms, our companies have never been better. No, they fail rather because of the inability of their managers to identify change in good time and to respond both courageously and energetically.

◆ The reasons for this are also clear from the survey. They are rooted in the personalities of managers ("alpha dogs" who are given to hubris and who lack self-reflection), internal cultures of "yes men" (i.e. an inability at the highest level to deal with conflicts) and a lack of team orientation (i.e. values are not lived out).

◆ Turning this perspective around and looking at what characterizes good management – management that successfully guides a company through its lifecycle – we zoomed in on three factors. These three factors increase the chances of steady growth: fortune, which favors the brave (a synonym for good ideas, creativity and good timing), outstanding management skills (operational excellence and avoiding diseconomies of scale) and above all the right personal leadership attributes, namely optimism, courage, a balanced perspective, trust, fairness and integrity.

The interviews that Mario Müller-Dofel conducted with Franz Fehrenbach, Jürgen Hambrecht, Wolfgang Reitzle and Alexander Rittweger confirm this conceptual analysis, I believe. The focus is not on commercial or economic models. Rather, the key theme of the interviews is: How do we achieve long-term alignment across all levels of the company? How do I get my people to want to follow me? How can I gain a better understanding of what concerns my teams, so that I can respond to them better – which again will get them to follow me? How do I get my messages across in such a way that my teams understand where I want them to go? Key issues here include trust, togetherness, intimacy, courage, optimism, collaboration and sustainability. In other words, it is the strength of management and the example it sets (assuming it is good at its job) that makes the difference.

This focus is consistent with the findings of our conceptual investigation: Good management means recognizing challenges, taking account of imponderables, setting ambitious goals, getting employees to buy into what you are doing, giving them a sense of security and triggering a positive dynamic. However, since words say more than a thousand analyses, here are a few quotes from the interviews that, for me, sum up exactly what good management means in today's world:

"When we realized in 2008 that we could forget our numbers-based planning, we switched to management by principles instead." (Fehrenbach)

"Company leaders need a telescope to track social, technological and regulatory developments. And they need a microscope to see what their company is currently able to achieve and what it will need to achieve in the future in light of these developments." (Hambrecht)

"[Company leaders] must also be prepared to say exactly what their company's position is, with ruthless, no-holds-barred honesty. Errors of self-perception are a common reason why companies fail." (Hambrecht)

"[For us,] focusing on the future takes precedence over focusing on profits." (Fehrenbach)

"The only way to contain the fear of overstretching yourself is to think through every conceivable negative scenario on a rational basis. Ultimately, though, it takes resolute courage to take a big step."(Reitzle)

"Managers are the ones who have to try to solve problems. Managers need to be able to look critically at themselves, which, sadly, we sometimes see too little of." (Hambrecht)

"I think it's often less a lack of courage on the part of employees that puts the brake on companies' dynamism and more the wrong reactions from management when things go wrong." (Fehrenbach)

"If you only ever act cautiously, you can't develop a company." (Reitzle)

"[You need to be able to] put up with huge frustrations. However hard the setbacks were, we always got back on our feet again." (Rittweger)

"One aspect of good management is not surrounding yourself with opportunists." (Reitzle)

"When you're the boss – be it in the startup phase or later on in the lifecycle – you always need intelligent opposition if you want to stay on track." (Rittweger)

"A company boss can't focus on keeping people comfortable." (Reitzle)

"Managers also need sufficient empathy to try to sense what's going on with their people. [I show respect by] extending [my] hand in welcome, addressing employees by name, looking them in the eye when I talk to them, pouring coffee for them." (Hambrecht)

4.2
AN AGENDA FOR GOOD MANAGEMENT

That leaves us with the second question raised by the quote from Lichtenberg with which I started this chapter: How will things get better? In other words: How can we get closer to the ideal of good management as I have tried to describe it? How do we ensure that managers maintain an excellent command of the tools of their trade in the long run? That lasting values are anchored in our companies? That an interdisciplinary mindset is cultivated? That strength of leadership genuinely sets an example for others? In response to these questions, I envisage an agenda for good management that should, at a bare minimum, include the following six points:

FIRST:
CHANGE THE EDUCATION PROVIDED BY UNIVERSITIES

If my suspicion that interdisciplinary thinking and the ability to think things through thoroughly will become increasingly important in the future, this must necessarily have repercussions for the education that we provide at our universities and business schools. I have never hidden my view that both a constant emphasis on a more practical orientation and the Bologna reform are wrong. Both have led to a situation in which we provide more training than education. And in the process, we doggedly teach the success factors of the past while the world changes and moves ahead ever faster.

I see only one option: We must challenge the universities to dare to teach more theory! This can be achieved by a three-way combination:

- A core curriculum that, in keeping with the Humboldt philosophy, builds a broad base at the beginning, laying philosophical foundations, incorporating values and communicating knowledge.
- Explicitly theoretical teaching that consciously focuses on theories, hypothetical concepts and analytical skills.
- A broad study base that, right from the outset, incorporates other disciplines and leaves sufficient time for them. Business management studies, for example, could be enriched by lectures in economics, politics and sociology.

My call for universities to dare to teach more theory also applies to the corporate community. When talking to top managers, I often find them quickly agreeing to the idea of more theory. Yet at the same time, the specialist and HR departments want young graduates with practical training who can be quickly deployed. Our universities must not be left to shoulder the burden alone. Companies too must ensure that young people who have opted for a theoretical education are given a fair chance. For me, daring to teach more theory also means that scientific excellence must take pride of place at our universities and institutes of higher education. If we want to make the most of the manufacturing skills that set Germany and Europe apart, and if we want to do so for a long time to come, we need more than just good engineers and scientists. We also need excellence in the science of economics and business. That doesn't simply mean that every university must now adopt a scientific focus. The diversity in today's education sector leaves room for various stances to be adopted. And that in turn leaves options open for those who see their skills and talents in more practical areas.

SECOND:
REINFORCE ON-THE-JOB DEVELOPMENT AND TRAINING

My plea for more theory at universities is linked to my conviction that the best way to learn practical skills is in practice. Development and training in companies have a crucial role to play. Fortunately, many companies have made great progress in this area in recent years.

To my mind, however, we can still go a step further. True, the primary focus must be on operational and company-specific knowledge and skills. But that does not mean that we have to do without a broad-based and interdisciplinary approach. It has never done engineers any harm to wrestle with economic theory. Nor has any business administrator suffered from learning a little about process technology. Both can undoubtedly benefit from the challenge of a core curriculum.

A number of leading companies are already introducing aspects of this philosophy in their corporate academies. Ours is the Roland Berger School of Strategy and Economics, whose very name makes it clear that our main focus is on an interdisciplinary approach that builds bridges between different areas of knowledge. For smaller companies, such solutions are normally not an option. One option is to step up their collaboration on specific topics with local universities and other institutes of higher education.

THIRD: CHANGE CORPORATE RECRUITING POLICIES

Some time ago, at a debate organized by Germany's Spiegel magazine at the Leipzig Graduate School of Management, the students gave unanimous support to my theories about an interdisciplinary, broad-based, diverse approach to studying. But they complained that corporate recruiting policies just don't work like that. What matters are the grades you achieve at high school and university, short periods of study, practical knowledge and appropriate internships. Picture-perfect résumés, in other words, but not the rough edges and sharp corners, the experience gathered in other walks of life that is so important to me.

Sadly, those students were right. I can perfectly understand how the routines work in HR and specialist departments. Given the masses of applications they receive for attractive positions, supposedly objective criteria that tend to err on the side of the mainstream can be a useful aid. But if we want to change something here, top managers must intervene personally and directly, influencing the definition of the "right" skill profiles and criteria, and getting involved in the selection process itself. Unless top managers sit face to face with their potential successors, take the time to talk to them, communicate their values and set a visible example, they will never get the junior managers they want.

FOURTH: STRIKE A BALANCE BETWEEN MANAGEMENT AND LEADERSHIP

Back in 2003, Henry Mintzberg wrote: "Most of us have become so enamored of 'leadership' that 'management' has been pushed into the background. Nobody aspires to being a good manager anymore; everybody just wants to be a great leader.

But the separation of management from leadership is dangerous. Just as management without leadership encourages an uninspired style, which deadens activities, leadership without management encourages a disconnected style, which promotes hubris."[40]

I quote Mintzberg at such length because I believe he has perfectly encapsulated one key cause of poor management. Many of us have allowed ourselves to be too strongly influenced by the Anglo-American concept of leadership, the glamour of being center-stage. In doing so, we have chosen to ignore that this attitude may come at a high price. The danger is that we simplify and polarize, underestimate risks and fail to think things through.

That is why I believe that presenting a confident case for a solid command of management tools and for solutions and improvements that will remain effective in the long term is part and parcel of good management – even if it sounds pedestrian and leaves little room for stars and showmen.

FIFTH: BEAT THE DRUM FOR GOOD MANAGEMENT

When asked by a young man whether he should study Business Ethics, the inimitable Austrian satirist Karl Kraus is said to have replied: "Well, you need to make your mind up which." His bon mot is over 100 years old, yet it still rings true today. The image and reputation of top managers is in a sorry state, and the financial crisis has significantly accelerated the deterioration.

That concerns me for two reasons. First, on a personal level. Like 95% of all managers, I feel I am being wrongfully blamed and criticized for the misdeeds of others. Second, such accusations are damaging because they undermine the importance of business in society.

It is vitally important for us to publically argue the case for good management, over and over again. We need to create awareness of how difficult good management is today, showing that mistakes happen. Rather than show misplaced solidarity, we must clearly distance ourselves from those whose misdemeanors are rooted in violations of the key principles of good management. If we fail to speak out, negative public opinion will wash up on the shores of our companies too, and that will only make IT harder to cultivate good management

SIXTH: DON'T TOLERATE COMPROMISE

The easiest way to improve our image and reputation is to rigorously run our day-to-day business on the basis of clearly defined values. That is why I have given this point on my agenda for good management the title "Don't tolerate compromise". The values I see as vital – honesty, credibility, reliability, integrity and responsibility – are easy to say and easy to write about, but they are not easy to put into practice.

We all know the situation: Someone is up for promotion. They have delivered excellent business results but they don't stand for the values that are important to us. How are we to decide in these circumstances? Should we give precedence to the short term, choose the candidate and go for rapid business development? Or should we set greater store by our values? I know full well that opportunism can be necessary, precisely when such decisions have to be made. Yet I have also learned that such opportunism can come back to haunt you. Why? Because the organization responds very sensitively, judging how serious you are about values precisely on such issues as these. In cases of doubt, therefore: Don't tolerate compromise.

In the long run, the management principles advocated many years ago by Peter Drucker carry far greater weight.[41] Good managers, Drucker wrote, first ask "What is good for the company?" and not "What is good for me?". It is not always easy to follow this principle. There are many gray areas, and it is easy to deceive oneself. Drucker's second management principle, however, can readily be implemented by anyone who is willing to do so: "Above all, good managers think and say 'we' instead of 'I'!" In other words, they do not stand for the egocentricity and hubris that we have identified as a key reason why companies fail.

It is important to note that this collective principle does not mean everyone has to cozy up to each other. The manager's job is not to be liked or to avoid rocking the boat. On the contrary: The issues at stake are the courage to adopt a clear stance and respect for the individual and his or her contribution.

With that, I conclude my agenda for good management – and draw this book to a close. Not every point I have raised is easy to apply in the cut and thrust of day-to-day business. But as a guide for good management, what it boils down to is three key attributes. To paraphrase Martin Hilb: a cool head, a warm heart and working hands.

Three key attributes, the bottom line for good management. A cool head, because analytical skills are of crucial importance when dealing with complexity. A warm heart, because if you want to manage and lead, you have to like people and be willing to accept responsibility. And working hands, because managing means working hard and shouldering risks.

NOTES AND REFERENCES

01 At the time this book was published, Burkhard Schwenker returned as CEO of Roland Berger Strategy Consultants.

02 Result of a keyword search on Amazon for new German or English books about corporate management published after July 2002.

03 Manager Magazin, the German business monthly, issue 01/2012.

04 Ibid.

05 See, for example, K. H. Biedenkopf, Komplexität und Kompliziertheit, in: Informatik-Spektrum 17, 1994, pp. 82-86; H. Rosa, Beschleunigung. Die Veränderung der Zeitstrukturen in der Moderne, Frankfurt/Main, 2005.

06 Albert Einstein, www.aphorismen-archiv.de.

07 Financial Times, "Welch rues short-term profit 'obsession'", March 12, 2009.

08 B. Tuchman, "The March of Folly: from Troy to Vietnam", 1984.

09 The Conference Board, Answering the CEO Challenge: How Quality Can Drive Profitable Growth Across the Organization, Ottawa, 2010.

10 B. Schwenker, "Deutschland baut um" series, Handelsblatt, Nov. 21, 2005, Nov. 28, 2005, Dec. 5, 2005, Dec. 12, 2005, Dec. 19, 2005, Dec. 27, 2005 and Jan. 2, 2006.

11 See, for example, R. D. Buzzell, B. T. Gale, The PIMS Principles, New York, 1987.

12 M. R. Porter, Wettbewerbsstrategie, Frankfurt/Main 1987.

13 T. J. Peters, R. H. Waterman, In Search of Excellence, New York, 1982.

14 Charlie Chaplin, www.aphorismen-archiv.de.

15 Forbes Magazine, July 1987.

16 A. de Geus, The Living Company, Boston, 1997.

17 C. Stadler, P. Wältermann, Die Jahrhundert-Champions, Stuttgart, 2012.

18 http://www.finanzen.net/Index/DAX/Historische-Zusammensetzung.

19 Based on C. Stadler, P. Wältermann, referencing data from EIM Business & Policy Research, an independent research organization in the Netherlands.

20 C. Stadler, P. Wältermann, p. 8 ff.

21 ZEW, Ursachen für das Scheitern junger Unternehmen in den ersten fünf Jahren ihres Bestehens, Mannheim, 2010.

22 D. L. Birch, The Job Creation Process, Cambridge, 1979, regarded as one of the first studies of young companies, arrives at similar percentages.

23 S. J. Chapman, T. S. Ashton, The size of business, mainly in the textile industry, in: Journal of the Royal Statistical Society, 1914; one of the first (known) comparisons of corporate and natural development.

24 Key works include D. J. Levinson et al, The Seasons of a Man's Life, New York, 1978, and J. R. Kimberly, R. H. Miles, The Organizational Life Cycle Issues in the Creation, Transformation and Decline of Organizations, San Francisco, 1980.

25 D. Miller, P. H. Friesen, Successful and unsuccessful phases of the corporate life cycle, in: Organization Studies, vol. 4, issue 4, 1983.
26 A. Ward, The Leadership Lifecycle, New York, 2003.
27 B. Schwenker, K. Spremann, Management between Strategy and Finance, Berlin/Heidelberg, 2008.
28 B. Schwenker, T. Raffel, Economic Scenario 2012, Munich, 2012.
29 For details of our initial studies, see B. Schwenker, S. Bötzel, Making Growth Work, Berlin/Heidelberg, 2007.
30 www.wissenfabrik.de. Backed by 100 companies in Germany, the "Knowledge Factory" promotes science and enterprise. To this end, startup founders and young entrepreneurs are supported by focused knowledge transfer and access to networks, for example.
31 The same goes for the "Enable2Start" startup competition run by Financial Times Deutschland, which regularly publishes compendiums detailing the development of the winning companies and also provides a very good insight into the fate of company founders (search for "enable2start" on Amazon).
32 See A. Ward, p. 25.
33 B. Schwenker, S. Bötzel, Auf Wachstumskurs, Berlin/Heidelberg, 2006.
34 The second management lie is: "The check is in the mail". In the interests of political correctness, the third one cannot be reproduced here.
35 B. Schwenker, Europe shows the way – The case for a successful management model, Cologne, 2011.
36 C. Stadler, P. Wältermann, p. 21 ff.
37 C. Stadler, P. Wältermann, p. 45 ff.
38 J. Shet, R. Sisodia, The Rule of Three: Why Only Three Major Competitors will Survive in any Market, New York, 2002.
39 B. Schwenker, Europe shows the way, p. 92 ff.
40 J. Gosling, H. Mintzberg, The Five Minds of a Manager, in: Harvard Business Review, November 2003, pp. 54-63.
41 W. W. Weber, G. Kulothungan (editors), Peter F. Drucker's Next Management, Göttingen, 2010.

ABOUT THE AUTHORS

PROF. DR. BURKHARD SCHWENKER

Prof. Dr. Burkhard Schwenker, born 1958, is CEO of Roland Berger Strategy Consultants. From August 2010 to May 2013, he served as Chairman of the international strategy consultancy, a function he took over from the company's founder Prof. Dr. h.c. Roland Berger. As of February 2012, Burkhard Schwenker was also appointed Chairman of the new Roland Berger School of Strategy and Economics (RBSE). He is a regular and acknowledged author in the field of corporate strategy and business policy and teaches strategic management at the Leipzig Graduate School of Management (HHL). In addition, he volunteers his time to serve as Chairman of the Roland Berger Foundation, Deputy Chairman of Atlantik Brücke e.V. and Chairman of the Board of the Hamburg Symphony Orchestra. He also sits on the Boards of Trustees of the World Wide Fund for Nature (WWF) and the Values Commission (Wertekommission e.V.) and is a member of the Senate of acatech, the German Academy of Science and Engineering.

MARIO MÜLLER-DOFEL

Mario Müller-Dofel, born 1972, is a business journalist, interviewer and communications/behavior coach. Following his studies at the Holtzbrinck School of Journalism, he worked for almost eight years at the Munich-based capital market magazine Euro, including two years as Copy Chief and Deputy Editor-in-Chief (until July 2012). While at the magazine he carried out in-depth interviews with around 100 CEOs, politicians and economists. His book "Interviews führen. Ein Handbuch für Ausbildung und Praxis" ("Interview techniques. A handbook for training and practice") was published by Econ Verlag in 2009. In 2011/2012 he trained as a communications and behavior coach at the artop Institute at the Humboldt University in Berlin. On November 1, 2012 he founded the training company DIALEKTIK for Business, based in Frankfurt (Main).

ABOUT RBSE

EXCELLENCE IN RESEARCH AND TEACHING

Roland Berger School of Strategy and Economics (RBSE) is the new corporate university of Roland Berger Strategy Consultants. It is where our consultants pool their knowledge, and the means by which they share it both within Roland Berger and with the outside world. We ensure hands-on knowledge transfer through high-quality courses, soon available to clients and business partners too. Our publications present the latest research findings and a unique store of methodological expertise.

RBSE's mission is to help business leaders master the complexities of corporate management and develop sustainable strategies. To achieve this mission, we analyze the latest trends in business and society and investigate their impact on the corporate community. In THOUGHTS, our series of publications for thought leaders, we provide a cross-industry and interdisciplinary angle on key issues that shape the future. RBSE collaborates closely with a global network of first-class academics to deliver on its promise of excellence in research and teaching.

www.rolandberger.com/rbse
rbse@rolandberger.com